Instructional Sequence Matters

Grades 3–5

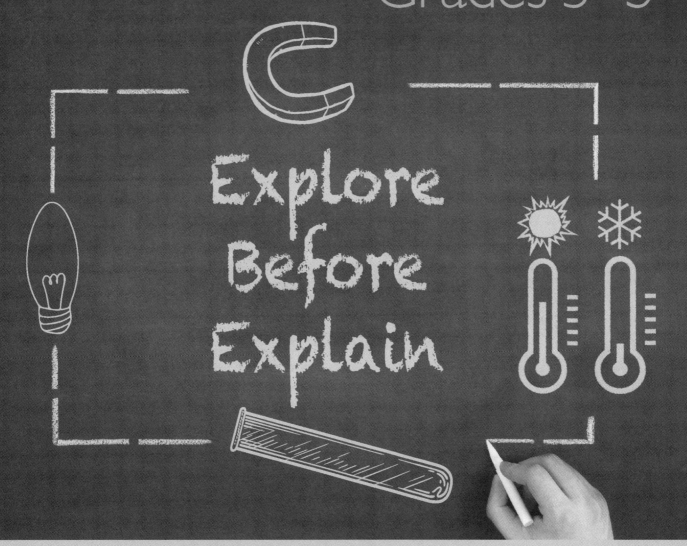

Explore
Before
Explain

Instructional Sequence Matters
Grades 3–5

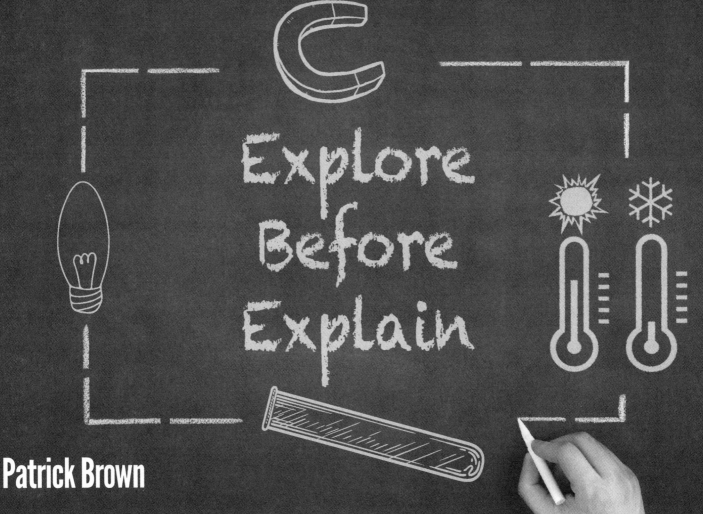

Explore Before Explain

Patrick Brown

NSTApress
National Science Teaching Association
Arlington, Virginia

National Science Teaching Association

Claire Reinburg, Director
Rachel Ledbetter, Managing Editor
Andrea Silen, Associate Editor
Jennifer Thompson, Associate Editor
Donna Yudkin, Book Acquisitions Manager

ART AND DESIGN
Will Thomas Jr., Director, cover and interior design

PRINTING AND PRODUCTION
Catherine Lorrain, Director

NATIONAL SCIENCE TEACHING ASSOCIATION
David L. Evans, Executive Director

1840 Wilson Blvd., Arlington, VA 22201
www.nsta.org/store
For customer service inquiries, please call 800-277-5300.

Library of Congress Cataloging-in-Publication Data
Names: Brown, Patrick, 1978- author.
Title: Instructional sequence matters, grades 3–5 : explore before explain / Patrick Brown.
Description: Arlington : National Science Teaching Association, [2020] | Includes bibliographical references and index.
Identifiers: LCCN 2019027257 (print) | LCCN 2019027258 (ebook) | ISBN 9781681406589 (paperback) | ISBN 9781681406596 (pdf)
Subjects: LCSH: Science--Study and teaching (Elementary)--United States.
Classification: LCC Q183.3.A1 B76844 2019 (print) | LCC Q183.3.A1 (ebook) | DDC 372.35/044--dc23
LC record available at *https://lccn.loc.gov/2019027257*
LC ebook record available at *https://lccn.loc.gov/2019027258*

To my favorite kid scientists: Finn, Lua, Bella, Charlie, Harry, Etta Mae, Penelope, Juliette, and Darby.

The more you read, the more things you will know.
The more things that you learn, the more places you will go.

—Dr. Seuss, *I Can Read With My Eyes Shut!* (Random House, 1978)

Contents

Foreword

From time to time, one identifies a new leader, someone the community has not recognized — yet. Then one goes to an NSTA conference and hears a presentation, joins a webinar, or reads an original book and realizes the leadership that is evident. This happened as I read *Instructional Sequence Matters, Grades 3–5: Explore Before Explain*.

Patrick Brown provides a wonderful book for science teachers. Not only is *Instructional Sequence Matters* a delightful read, it also is practical and helpful. What more could science teachers ask for? After starting with chapters on students' development and learning, modern sequences of instruction (including the 5E Instructional Model), and the synthesis of science concepts and practices, Dr. Brown describes various instructional strategies, such as demonstrations, readings, investigations, videos, and lectures, all components of integrated instructional sequences. The bulk of the book illustrates what it means to effectively teach science concepts such as heat and temperature, magnetism, and electric circuits.

Through the narrative and examples, Dr. Brown encourages teachers to change their mind-set about their instructional sequence. Using terms from the 5E Instructional Model (Bybee 2015), Dr. Brown demonstrates what it means to think about and apply *explore-before-explain* as a mind-set for teaching. Why did he embrace this mind-set? In his career, Dr. Brown observed and subsequently conducted research on preservice science teachers who had difficulty embracing the 5E Instructional Model because it was very different from their experiences and subsequent images of teachers and teaching and their successes as science students.

The rationale for using *explore-before-explain* as a mind-set also recognizes the importance of students constructing claims based on evidence before teachers provide explanations of science phenomena.

Finally, the examples help the reader address the dimensions of science and engineering practices, crosscutting concepts, and disciplinary core ideas as presented in the *Next Generation Science Standards* (*NGSS*) and many contemporary state science standards. Each example of an instructional sequence has clear connections to the *NGSS* and the *Common Core State Standards*.

In the final chapter, "Leadership and Lessons Learned," Dr. Brown lists lessons for teachers — for example, focus on science phenomena, emphasize *explore-before-explain* teaching, plan 5E (Engage, Explore, Explain, Elaborate, Evaluate) and POE (Predict, Observe, and Explain) lessons that incorporate *NGSS* domains, and recognize that changing one's mind-set about teaching takes time and conscious effort.

Foreword

I was originally drawn to this book because of Dr. Brown's use of the 5E Instructional Model. Reading *Instructional Sequence Matters* reinforced my first engagement with the book. Soon, however, I found other compelling reasons to recommend this book to all science teachers. The book is written by a teacher for teachers, it provides model lessons with a personal narrative that includes the decisions Dr. Brown himself had to make as a teacher, and it weaves in connections from the three dimensions of the *NGSS*. Finally, the book uses the 5E Model and presents descriptions of the model with insightful examples. Without any hesitation, I recommend this book.

—Rodger W. Bybee
Author of *The BSCS 5E Instructional Model:*
Creating Teachable Moments (NSTA Press, 2015)

Acknowledgments

Developing *Instructional Sequence Matters, Grades 3–5* required a close look at the research supporting *explore-before-explain* teaching in the elementary grades and the *Next Generation Science Standards*. Many thanks to Dr. Rodger Bybee, Dr. Janice Koch, and Deborah Siegel, whose conversations encouraged me to write a companion book specific for elementary school teachers. My appreciation also goes to Claire Reinburg, Rachel Ledbetter, Andrea Silen, and Jennifer Thompson at the National Science Teaching Association (NSTA) for their outstanding editorial and production work. I give special thanks to the reviewers, who did a phenomenal job providing feedback on earlier versions of this manuscript: Peter Bernson, Anne Tweed, Wendy Frazier, and Andrea Foster. The manuscript is better for NSTA's support and talents.

About the Author

Dr. Patrick L. Brown is the executive director of STEM and career education for the Fort Zumwalt School District in St. Charles, Missouri. Before arriving at Fort Zumwalt, he received a PhD in curriculum and instruction from the University of Missouri, Columbia.

Dr. Brown has a range of K–12 and postsecondary teaching experience. He has taught elementary-level, middle-level, and high school lessons. In addition, he has taught both undergraduate and graduate courses for prospective elementary, middle, and high school teachers. Dr. Brown has won various awards for his science methods course teaching.

Dr. Brown makes frequent presentations at international, regional, and state conferences and is known for his scholarship on instructional sequences to teach science. His science teaching ideas have appeared in *Science and Children*, *Science Scope*, *The Science Teacher*, and *Science Activities*. His research in science education has been published in *Science Education*, the *Journal of Science Teacher Education*, and the *International Journal of Science Education*.

Preface

Instructional Sequence Matters, Grades 3–5 is intended for elementary school educators, both new and experienced, as well as subject matter specialists, curriculum coordinators, and preservice and inservice trainers interested in enhancing student learning and motivation through simple shifts in their instructional practices. I provide numerous examples throughout the book about why instructional sequence matters from a pedagogical perspective and include many model lessons tied to contemporary national standards.

This book is intended to be the companion to Instructional Sequence Matters, Grades 6–8. I provide elementary teachers with a good balance between the theoretical foundations of effective teaching and learning and practical, classroom-tested instructional activities. As you will learn, Instructional Sequence Matters is all about explore-before-explain teaching, which is not a prescribed program but a way of thinking more purposefully and carefully about the nature of how we design instruction. While there are many changes and additions in this elementary-level version of the book, its philosophy and structure stay the same as the middle-level book. I wanted to keep some of the core examples and strategies that have stood the test of time and that I have used with elementary students. I had good reasons for keeping the model lessons the same as in the middle-level book: First, they were favorites among elementary students. And second, they all lead to students developing long-lasting understanding.

This book builds on Instructional Sequence Matters, Grades 6–8 to meet some of the unique needs of elementary educators. I continue to suggest ways to advance students' science thinking in this book, grounded in the scholarship of teaching and learning. I include a mostly new chapter devoted to research on young children through adolescents. Many emerging bodies of research emphasize the importance of explore-before-explain teaching and expand on what we know about how people learn.

This companion book continues to illustrate the seamless translation of explore-before-explain teaching and the three dimensions of the Next Generation Science Standards (NGSS Lead States 2013): (1) science and engineering practices, (2) disciplinary core ideas, and (3) crosscutting concepts. These standards are described and closely connected to every aspect of the model lessons illustrating key physical science topics.

Finally, elementary teachers have to be picky about what they choose to read and how they teach, because they often work in a crowded school day where every instructional minute counts. I would challenge you to consider that explore-before-explain teaching can be so much more than a science lesson planning tool, and it lends empirical support for the placement of other experiences in the elementary classroom to leverage the best possible learning experiences for students. As you will learn, one of

Preface

the hallmarks of *explore-before-explain* teaching is its emphasis on learning for understanding and wiring (or rewiring) the brain, so knowledge is deeply blanketed in evidence-based experiences. You will learn that using *explore-before-explain* teaching is an investment in student learning that can pay off big dividends. Teachers can use the context that science creates, and the brain-friendly development promoted by *explore-before-explain* teaching, to take students' interdisciplinary learning to higher levels. These assertions are supported by cognitive science research that emphasizes the critical importance of students' prior knowledge and how it is organized and expanded through cumulative learning experiences (Bransford, Brown, and Cocking 2000).

I have been gratified over the years by the number of positive responses I have received from elementary teachers and how their use of *explore-before-explain* practices with students has taken all learning to new levels. Even more rewarding than teacher compliments are the shared classroom memories from former elementary students who, as high school students and beyond, remember their *explore-before-explain* experiences in learning science.

Introduction

If I have seen further, it is by standing on the shoulders of giants.
—Isaac Newton (1675)

Students come to us as knowers. They have lived a few years and have constructed ideas about how the world works. They are puzzled when rainbows appear in the sky, when the leaves change colors, and when the Moon goes through different phases. Their observations can lead to questions about how the world works. Ever curious about their world, children instinctively try to answer their scientifically oriented questions by looking for patterns and causal relationships.

When they learn about the world, children do not just hit the right answers all at once. They develop ideas by building on previous experiences. There is a continuous advancement of thoughts, ideas, and sense-making. They correct errors in their thinking and revise misconceptions based on experiences. Their learning is not just dependent on the knowledge they construct entirely through self-discoveries. They receive explanations to help them understand the world. I firmly believe that a significant task of science teaching is cultivating the innate skills that child scientists bring to school and balancing their ideas with purposeful pedagogical practices. Bringing an *explore-before-explain* mind-set to science teaching is a way to develop the budding scientist in each of your students.

An *explore-before-explain* mind-set honors that students naturally develop ideas all on their own while it also highlights our essential role in their development. The framework is not a prescribed method, nor an advertisement for an entirely discovery-based approach to learning. It would not be necessary for students to rediscover all knowledge, which in many cases took scientists hundreds of years to invent. (This is applying the "standing on the shoulders of giants" idea to our important role as *explore-before-explain* teachers!) *Explore-before-explain* learning highlights a unique synergy between explorations and explanations, and it recognizes that explorations need to come first. Students' ideas and skills are powerful forces that drive intellectual development. Equally fundamental is how we provide explanations in light of students' life experiences. All learning is cumulative, and individuals' experiences as knowers—along with their interactions with teachers (and other adults, of course)—pave the way for developing a more sophisticated understanding. ("If I have seen further" is an implication of an *explore-before-explain* mind-set in the type of classroom culture of learning that we want to create for our students.)

Two contemporary ways to put an *explore-before-explain* mind-set into practice are the favored POE (Predict, Observe, and Explain) and BSCS 5E (Engage, Explore,

Introduction

Explain, Elaborate, Evaluate) instructional models. The POE and 5E instructional models sequence science instruction, so students explore science before elaborating their understanding from explanations. Both came from the three-phase 1960s science learning cycle (Atkin and Karplus 1962; Bybee 1997). In addition, the POE and 5E models allow students to construct content knowledge using science practices, a productive approach that mirrors how science is done in the real world. Later chapters will cover the similarities and differences among the learning cycle, POE, and 5E. These approaches are not a curriculum but a way to sequence activities so they align with how students learn best. If you are already aware of the power of the POE and 5E instructional models, this book may help you reflect on ways to make instruction even more effective for students. However, I hope it will do more than that. Others have written about using the 5E and POE models in teaching (see Abell and Volkmann 2006; Haysom and Bowen 2010). My approach is consistent with their ideas, but at the same time, it is unique.

A New Mind-Set for Approaching Science Teaching

We are all designers by nature, but how we strategize our planning practices can significantly facilitate the change we want to see in our lessons. As we embark on our journey, we will distinguish between *explore-before-explain* and 5E or POE teaching, because once we develop this mind-set, it drastically influences how we think about instructional design. While the details are soon to come, *explore-before-explain* teaching is all about creating conceptual coherence for learners. If we can begin our planning by thinking about the experiences students could have that would allow them to construct some accurate science knowledge, we can more easily situate learning around phenomena, decide explanations necessary for students as the science storyline unfolds, and offer elaborations to sophisticate student understanding.

I also highlight *explore-before-explain* teaching because it is not a predominating practice. A look into typical classrooms shows that hands-on activities have a standard script in U.S. classrooms where teacher explanation comes first, followed by verification and practice-type activities (Hofstein and Lunetta 2004). This type of approach fails to promote the kind of logical and critical thinking about data that can be used as evidence to explain science. In addition, this sequence does little to help students overcome inaccurate ideas and misconceptions that may be grounded in what could seem reasonable, but are unsubstantiated by empirical evidence and not an accurate depiction of science (Duschl, Schweingruber, and Shouse 2007). To help students develop knowledge by doing science, the National Research Council (NRC 2012) has suggested that they need to learn core ideas in different science disciplines (physical science, Earth and space science, and life science); be able to use the seven crosscutting concepts to think logically about data, evidence, and phenomena; and participate in eight science and engineering practices that allow for the construction of more accurate science knowledge.

While we will delve into the particulars of these essential practices, crosscutting concepts, and disciplinary ideas in later chapters, the motive for the change is three-fold. First, as you will come to learn, students have a lot of room to grow. Second, students need to be the ones doing the hard intellectual work in the classroom to be prepared for the new trends, challenges, and skills necessary for global competitiveness in a changing workforce landscape. Finally, we need some new ways of thinking about teaching, to prepare students for their ever-changing world.

So why the change, and why now? Underlying the answer to this question are national and international assessments that seem to indicate that our students are not gaining proficiencies in science. These tests attempt to quantify students' preparedness for future schooling and for life. The National Assessment of Educational Progress (NAEP) assesses what students know and what they can do in different subject areas. Only 21% of students demonstrate science proficiency on the NAEP by 12th grade (U.S. Department of Education 2015). The ACT recently developed metrics to project potential success in different college science programs. According to the ACT (2015), merely 38% of students met or surpassed the science benchmark.

Students' potential to do better is similar to international tests. The Programme for International Student Assessment (PISA) measures students' abilities to think critically and solve problems in math, science, and reading. Results of the PISA test (from 2000, 2003, 2006, 2009, and 2012) demonstrate that U.S. students rank from 34% to 55% against students from other countries assessed in science (Organisation for Economic Co-operation and Development 2012). Meanwhile, the Trends in International Mathematics and Science Study (TIMSS) evaluates students' science and mathematics achievement. The latest TIMSS findings indicate that fourth- and eighth-grade U.S. students were ranked 11th and 12th, respectively, of all countries tested (International Association for the Evaluation of Educational Achievement 2015).

My point here is not to provide an exhaustive list of statistics on how our students perform, but to suggest that our lackluster results show a continuing shortfall in students' preparedness. Whether the assessment is looking at students' abilities to answer specific content questions or evaluating their logical thinking and reasoning abilities, we still have a long way to go. The results of national and international tests, as well as the outcomes of misconception research, indicate that we need a new way to think about teaching and learning. Now is the time to ask yourself, are you up for the challenge?

A General Overview for Using This Book

This book provides a self-guided professional development experience (see the Activity Box, pp. xx–xxi). The activities that follow will help you with national reform aimed at putting *A Framework for K–12 Science Education* (NRC 2012) and the *Next Generation Science Standards* (*NGSS*; NGSS Lead States 2013) into practice.

Introduction

Activity Box:
Promoting Professional Development and Professional Learning Communities

The activity boxes throughout this book are meant to provide a professional development experience and promote job-embedded learning. Part of my hope is that your learning is ongoing and extends beyond the knowledge gleaned from reading this book and that you will try the model lessons and use the design practices to create your own *explore-before-explain* experiences. As with your students who benefit from *explore-before-explain* teaching, you will find that many of the lessons require learning by doing. One difference is that I have structured the book so an explanation of learning theory and instructional sequence is up-front. You might try to do a model lesson first, before diving deep into the research sections that start with Chapter 1. (This would be an *explore-before-explain* approach to your professional development!)

We can increase our learning by collectively working together. A professional learning community (PLC) is dedicated to working collaboratively to improve learning for students. If we use PLCs to collaborate, we need to establish some parameters for our work:

- *What are the expectations of the group?*
  Representative activities: How will the team decide on group norms? Will the team be establishing group member roles?

- *What are the expectations for student learning? What sources will be drawn on when we decide on our expectations for learning?* Representative activities: How will science standards drive our expectations for student learning? Can we use science as a vehicle for developing a student's proficiency in the *Common Core State Standards*? If so, what standards will we draw on to reinforce our work?

- *What results will we focus on to determine whether our approaches are leading to higher levels of learning and motivation?*
  Representative activities: Can we use common pretests and posttests to assess students' development of understanding? What performance tasks might help us know whether students have

gained the necessary proficiencies in science content and practices? Can students track their science content and practices development (i.e., can we promote a metacognitive approach)?

- *How will we measure the effectiveness of our PLC?*
Representative activities: Can we measure our adherence to *explore-before-explain* teaching by looking at similarities and differences between our past and current lessons? Can we offer lessons studies where we observe each other's *explore-before-explain* lessons?

My goal is that teachers will read the chapters, reflect on their practices, learn from the examples, and use the design principles to start creating 5E and POE lessons that align with the *NGSS*. This book draws heavily from the research on effective professional development that highlights the critical role of active learning in context and explicit reflection in practice (Reiser 2013). Also, research from *The Cambridge Handbook of Expertise and Expert Performance* recognized that developing knowledge is most meaningful if it is integrated into practice (Ericsson et al. 2006). Thus, to become experts, teachers will need time to think about the sequence of science instruction and the *NGSS*, and they probably will not be perfect right at the start.

Each chapter of this book grew out of research experiences, from working with elementary students, and through teacher preparation and professional development. I have embedded activities aimed at sparking your thinking about your own experiences and designing *explore-before-explain* instructional sequences (see the activity boxes throughout the chapters). I learned through research that teachers can have difficulty embracing the 5E Instructional Model because this instructional sequence is different from their experiences as students and their mind-set toward science teaching (see Brown, Friedrichsen, and Abell 2013). Success in K–16 science experiences can provide robust ideas about what science teaching could look like and how to best prepare students to develop their understanding.

You can use the discussion questions in this book to reflect on, both individually and with colleagues, your beliefs about science teaching and experiences as a learner. Our experiences as learners, current work with students, and beliefs about effective instruction can be compelling evidence for our ideas and inform our future practices. During the reading activities, make note of ideas so you can easily reflect on their initial discussions after experiencing model lessons. The combination of reflection questions, research chapters, and model lessons strongly supports an *explore-before-explain* mind-set.

In Chapter 1, "Rethinking Development and Learning," I start with the research on learning and cognition. This chapter takes you through some of the emerging ideas

Introduction

about students' intellectual abilities in terms of developmental psychology, neuroscience, and cognitive science research and the implications for the instructional sequence.

Chapter 2, "Connecting Hands-On With Minds-On Experiences," shows why the exact placement of activities in instruction is pivotal in learning. I compare two different hands-on approaches. I support the assertions about why *explore-before-explain* teaching is beneficial for learners with abundant science education research that can be further explored.

Chapter 3, "Modern Sequences of Instruction," discusses the key components of two contemporary sequences of science instruction. You will read about the phases of the POE and 5E instructional models. The activity boxes are aimed at helping you reflect on hands-on practices you currently use and how they may be sequenced to promote even higher levels of learning.

In Chapter 4, "Content and Process Working Together," I describe the construction of the *NGSS*. I share some activities for you to reflect on the lessons you currently use and the connections to components of the *NGSS*.

Next, in Chapter 5, "Where to Start," I provide guidance on how you can create 5Es that translate the *NGSS*. I present activities following each factor that you should consider when planning 5Es and offer some planning ideas to design *explore-before-explain* instructional sequences based on cognitive science research.

In Chapters 6–13, I share grades 3–5 model lessons for putting the *explore-before-explain* mind-set into practice using either a POE or a 5E instructional sequence in physical science, life science, and Earth and space science. I offer the lessons from the different disciplines from a grade-span perspective because how you cluster standards to make learning meaningful for students is vital. As you will come to see, the *explore-before-explain* activities create the science storyline and the gradual unfolding of related ideas. Occasionally, standards across the grade span are touched on or addressed at an earlier grade than recommended by the *NGSS* to build students' conceptual coherence. The model lessons illustrate how both the POE and 5E models easily translate into the *NGSS*. Also, the narrative portions of the model lessons are coded with specific elements of the *NGSS* (NGSS Lead States 2013, Appendixes F and G). An *NGSS* summary table is provided to show the close connection between student actions and *NGSS* dimensions. The model lessons allow you to see the POE or 5E model and the *NGSS* in action.

Chapter 14, "Leadership and Lessons Learned," takes you through five key points for putting an *explore-before-explain* mind-set into practice using POE and 5E sequences and the *NGSS*. This final chapter can help emphasize the steps necessary for supporting colleagues and developing collaborative teams interested in shepherding the POEs and 5Es into practice.

Conclusions

Teacher educators and professional developers can easily implement these lessons to model best practices in science education. Beginning teachers can use the model lessons so they have research-based strategies to improve student learning during their first years of teaching. Experienced teachers who already value hands-on approaches but find that their lessons fall slightly short in influencing students the way they intended can benefit from simple reorganizing activities. Reading and discussing the chapters provides valuable insight into why some approaches may be more beneficial than others. Thus, teachers have real-life examples and a rationale for restructuring the hands-on approaches they are currently using. Regardless of the level of experience, from novice to expert teacher, educators can read, implement, and dissect each model lesson to help reflect on how the sequence of science instruction promotes long-lasting understanding.

The chapters build on one another so you can consider why some activities may be even more effective than others and so you can try them out with your students. Many teachers realize that simple shifts in the arrangement and combination of activities can positively affect student learning. In addition, effective science teaching is not always about working harder—it is about working smarter. Reflecting on and experiencing exploration before explanation instructional sequences opens up opportunities to construct a theoretical model for classroom lesson design so that all students gain higher levels of science literacy.

A NOTE ON SAFETY

Science teaching necessarily involves working with different materials, and at times, this can pose safety hazards. Safety *always* needs to be the first concern in all of our teaching. Teachers need to be sure that their rooms and other spaces are appropriate for the activities being conducted. That means that engineering controls such as proper ventilation, a fire extinguisher, and an eye-wash station—and appropriate personal protective equipment (PPE) such as safety goggles or safety glasses with side shields and gloves—are available and used properly. In addition, there should be sanitized, indirectly vented chemical-splash goggles or safety glasses with side shields as appropriate, nonlatex aprons, and vinyl gloves during all components of investigations (i.e., the setup, hands-on investigation, and cleanup) when students are using potentially harmful supplies, equipment, or chemicals.

At a minimum, the eye protection PPE provided for students to use must meet the ANSI/ISEA Z87.1 D3 standard. Remember to review and comply with all safety policies and procedures, including appropriate chemical management, that have been established by your school district. Teachers must also practice the proper disposal of materials, even common items such as baking soda and vinegar, as well as the proper maintenance of all equipment.

Continued

Introduction

The National Science Teaching Association maintains an excellent website (*www.nsta.org/safety*) that provides guidance for teachers at all levels. The site also has a safety acknowledgment form (sometimes called a "safety contract") that is specifically for elementary students to review with their teachers and have signed by parents or guardians (see *http://static.nsta.org/pdfs/SafetyAcknowledgmentForm-ElementarySchool.pdf*).

It cannot be overstated that safety is the single most important part of any lesson. Safety notes are included throughout this book to highlight specific concerns that might be associated with a particular lesson.

The safety precautions associated with each investigation are based, in part, on the use of recommended materials and instructions, legal safety standards, and better professional safety practices. The selection of alternative materials or procedures for these investigations may jeopardize the level of safety and therefore is at the user's own risk. Remember that an investigation includes three parts: (1) the setup, which is what you do to prepare the materials for students to use; (2) the actual investigation, which involves students using the materials and equipment; and (3) the cleanup, which includes cleaning the materials and putting them away for later use. The safety procedures and PPE stipulated for each investigation apply to all three parts.

Chapter 1

Rethinking Development and Learning

Chapter 1

This first chapter rests on a single premise with far-reaching implications: If we want to produce more powerful learning for students, then we need to ground our practice in current research on teaching and learning. What we know about students' intellectual abilities and knowledge development is much different from what it was 20 or 30 years ago. Students bring ideas to the classroom that are abstract and sophisticated. Children form complex ideas about how the world works based on direct experiences with their environment. From a very early age, kids observe their settings and are inquisitive about the natural world and their surroundings. They ask questions based on their experiences and actively seek out answers to their questions. Students form rudimentary theories using basic statistics and probability, and they develop principles to describe how the world works. Advances in developmental psychology, neuroscience, and cognitive science lend valuable insights into what kids can do when they come to school.

Developmental Psychology

Within developmental psychology there are many different theories about how young children and even babies understand the world, take in information, and advance over time. However, we learn that in just the brief years before school, there are enormous changes in children's ability to know and analyze the world around them. While there are remarkable differences between what young kids know and the analytical process they use to understand their surroundings, children at all ages tackle complex problems. Their understandings of these problems and their abilities to learn are dependent on their experiences. The point here is not to develop a detailed description of the cognitive differences that occur in the few years before children enter school, but to look across the different ages and see that there are some common basic ideas.

Studies on the cognition of early learning show that kids' play is an attempt to understand the way scientists do things through experimentation (Gopnik, Meltzoff, and Kuhl 1999). Young children investigate natural phenomena, have questions about the ways objects and things work, and collect information. Children use intelligence-gathering practices to learn about science. They form a hypothesis that is tested against the evidence, and the evidence makes them revise the hypothesis. All the while, young children are relying on pattern recognition and cause-and-effect relationships to develop a deeper understanding. This iterative hypothesis testing involves calculations with conditional probability. From a statistical perspective, young children learn about the likelihood of something happening based on another event occurring. Their learning is rapid where new understanding is dependent on prior data-producing experiences. Developmental research shows that young children can draw rich inferences from sparse data in a short amount of time (Gopnik, Meltzoff, and Kuhl 1999).

The developmental literature presents a noticeable departure from earlier views that assumed kids pass through concrete stages of intellectual development and can gain certain abilities only by getting older (Duschl, Schweingruber, and Shouse 2007). The literature simply has not supported the premise of rigid stages of development. Stagelike phases of cognitive development ignore students' inborn curiosity and problem-solving abilities, as well as the central role that active and supportive instruction plays in learning (Bransford, Brown, and Cocking 2000).

Just think, even tiny babies who cannot yet talk or walk use reasoning and critical thinking through their tactile experiences and analysis of data to learn about their environment. The world is not static, and movement provides clues about whether objects begin and end and the factors that influence the trajectory, speed, and momentum of an object (in other words, basic physics concepts). Imagine a baby rolling a ball across the floor in a room. The room may have many different factors that influence how balls will roll, such as carpeted and noncarpeted areas, walls, furniture, and other toys. In the same way, each of these factors provides its own unique learning experience from which babies construct knowledge. They pay attention to this sort of information to learn about their surroundings, and they are building fundamental physics ideas with little to no instruction from adults. Insights from the developmental research demonstrate that students' capabilities make it possible to create an innovative curriculum that addresses science content and practices and advances reasoning at a very early age.

Neuroscience

How we design instruction should also relate to what we know about how the brain develops over time. Until quite recently, understanding the mind, and thinking and learning, was limited by our technological abilities. By being able to look into the mechanisms of brain function and structure using imaging technologies (structural and functional MRIs), science has progressed from the prevailing thought that the majority of brain development occurs in the first few years of life to better understanding brain development across the life span. The revolution in the study of neuroscience has important implications for education. While there is some debate about

Chapter 1

the extent to which new neurons generate, because the majority of them are present at birth and the brain grows to about full size by age 6 (90% of adult volume), the connections between neurons—called synapses—are of utmost importance for understanding knowledge structures (Stiles and Jernigan 2010). In fact, studies show that the synapses proliferate after birth into childhood and then slow down in the later parts of adolescence and beyond (Blakemore 2010; Blakemore and Choudhury 2006).

From a neurobiological standpoint, early childhood learning experiences are essential because these learning experiences serve to create knowledge structures in the brain. Synapses that are being used are strengthened, while those that are not being used or are not particularly helpful are pruned away. The process is analogous to pruning a rose bush, in which the weaker branches are removed (pruned away) so the more significant branches can grow stronger. Synaptic pruning is a way to streamline neural circuits to boost knowledge and skills for adulthood. Although neural pruning may decline after adolescence, adults compensate by recruiting different neural mechanisms, and they tap into their lived experiences to problem solve and learn. According to the National Academies of Sciences, Engineering, and Medicine (NASEM),

> *The brain continues to adapt as the learner ages, through the continuous shaping and reshaping of neural connections in response to stimuli and demands. While the learner gains knowledge and skills as the brain develops throughout childhood and adolescence, the relationship between brain development and learning is not unidirectional: learning and brain development interact reciprocally. Learning changes the brain throughout the lifespan; at the same time, the brain develops throughout the lifespan in ways that influence learning and are in turn influenced by the learner's context and cultural influences.* (NASEM 2018, p. 3)

In sum, individuals continue to learn throughout their life span, and their early learning and brain development influence future learning and brain development (in other words, learning shapes the brain and vice versa). Insights from neuroscience clearly have education ramifications, because learning environments change the physical structure and functional organization of the brain. Advances in neuroscience research might revolutionize what we know about how teaching and learning environments influence brain development.

Cognitive Science

Forming effective instruction should also directly relate to the cognitive science research on what we know about the best possible learning environments. The books *How People Learn* (Bransford, Brown, and Cocking 2000) and *How People Learn II: Learners, Contexts, and Cultures* (NASEM 2018) describe three interrelated factors that are essential for ensuring high-quality classroom instruction: learner, knowledge, and assessment.

Learner-Centered

Fundamental to the idea of learner-centeredness is the idea that all knowledge is constructed through active experience. This means that knowledge is not passively received. The learner-centered principle is rooted in a long-held constructivist episte- mology that acknowledges that students learn science best when they actively construct knowledge that builds on prior understanding and that is based on firsthand experi- ences with data and evidence. Scholars who studied cognitive development, such as Jean Piaget, Jerome Bruner, and Lev Vygotsky, developed our primary understanding of learners and learning. This seems like a simple idea, but in fact, it is not. The best active, learner-centered lessons provide experiences that deeply entrench ideas and promote long-lasting understanding. In this regard, the understanding is highlighted by an individual's ability to reconstruct and apply conceptual knowledge rather than the retrieval of specific facts (NASEM 2018). Long-lasting understanding is promoted when learners construct knowledge, connect details within a broader framework for understanding, and relate information with the knowledge they already have.

Learner-centered environments are mediated by teachers and student-to-student experiences that make thinking and learning explicit for students. Learner-centered instruction describes a complex interaction among a student's prior knowledge and experiences, new individual and group experiences, and the student's own reflection and thinking about his or her developing understanding (the last concept is termed *metacognition*). Students come to school as knowers even before being taught anything. They have lived for some years and constructed ideas about how the world works. They have become knowers through their firsthand experiences that provide evidence for their ideas. The ideas they have constructed serve as the framework from which they try to advance their understanding. How students think about their ideas, and how they monitor and reflect on their developing understanding, is critical for their regulating and being more self-reliant learners (NASEM 2018).

If students' knowledge is rooted in alternative conceptions, it can become a barrier to future learning. The K–8 science education literature provides a litany of examples of students holding inaccurate ideas about science. These include broad thoughts and many specific, more nuanced ideas involving life and living processes (e.g., living things, nutrition, genetics, inheritance); materials and their properties (e.g., solids, liq- uids, and gases; chemical changes; particles); and physical processes (e.g., electricity, magnetism, energy) (see Driver et al. 1994). Examples of students' prior knowledge are well documented in the research literature. This is also a theme of many National Science Teaching Association books targeted at uncovering K–12 students' ideas (see Keeley, Eberle, and Dorsey 2008; Keeley, Eberle, and Farrin 2005; Keeley, Eberle, and Tugel 2007; Keeley and Tugel 2009). Because students' incoming ideas serve as the foundation for future learning, they are a critical consideration in planning. Evidence- based experiences and reflecting on developing understanding can help students overcome misconceptions. Learner-centered environments help students construct accurate understanding from data-producing experiences, along with interactions with teachers and peers.

Finally, the learner-centeredness of an environment is influenced by the upbringing of the individual. How learners grow and learn is related to their cultural, social cognitive, and biological contexts (NASEM 2018). Learning is influenced in fundamental ways by students' home environments, and the difficulties they encounter may be a mismatch between a student's cultural experience and the expectations at school. The cultural influence on learning goes beyond *what* students learn to include *how* they learn (Brown and Abell 2007a). Thus, classrooms should be learner-centered environments that highlight activating students' prior knowledge and engaging them in active experiences that promote thinking about developing understanding.

Knowledge-Centered

If, as learners, we all try to fit new experiences with prior knowledge, it follows that we learn most readily if the targeted ideas fit in a broader framework for what we should know and be able to do at a specific grade level or band. Knowledge-centered classrooms focus on the types of ideas, practices, and skills that students will encounter and how these ideas will be organized to optimize learning. The process of creating knowledge-centered classrooms requires us to evaluate our teaching environment. Essential questions come to mind when assessing the knowledge-centeredness of our science classrooms: (1) Is the subject matter aligned with the appropriate standards? (2) Is the topic connected to bigger, overarching ideas? (3) Is skill development focused on advancing abilities and how to use them over time?

The knowledge that students should gain at different ages and grade levels is well researched. In the past three decades in the United States, there have been no fewer than three significant reform documents in science education: *Benchmarks for Science Literacy* (American Association for the Advancement of Science 1993), *National Science Education Standards* (National Research Council 1996), and *Next Generation Science Standards* (NGSS Lead States 2013). Each of these reform documents used current research on science teaching and learning to set goals for the types of knowledge, skills, and abilities that students should gain from classroom instruction. A knowledge-centered environment introduces components of knowledge (e.g., concepts, facts, skills, reflection on thinking) promptly when the need for knowledge emerges or students need them. A knowledge-centered environment guides students in learning for long-lasting understanding and helps them transfer their abilities to new and different areas.

Assessment-Centered

Finally, teaching for optimal understanding requires an assessment-centered classroom. These classrooms focus on high standards for learning and frequent feedback so that students can self-monitor their developing understanding at all stages of development. Feedback comes in many forms and includes the assessment of students' development of ideas within a discipline of study (e.g., science content and practices used to generate knowledge) and becoming more independent learners. Also, feedback comes at different points in time during the learning process.

The importance of feedback is the subject of many resources for teachers. For instance, in *Understanding by Design*, Wiggins and McTighe (2005) argue that learning goals and assessments should be developed before designing instructional activities. Their backward design framework attempts to help teachers home in on essential knowledge in a unit of study and then design activities to help students learn new ideas and develop their abilities. Formative feedback is ongoing and used to help students monitor their developing understanding and take measures of what they have learned and what areas they still find confusing. Summative feedback helps teachers and students determine whether individuals and the classes as a whole have gained knowledge at the end of a unit of study. Assessment-centered classrooms help students isolate the knowledge and skills to develop so they can reach their peak academic abilities.

The Classroom Learning Culture

The principles underlying *How People Learn* and *How People Learn II* do not operate in isolation but are overlapping and deeply entrenched in one another to form the learning culture of the classroom (see Figure 1.1, p. 8). While I have described them as separate entities, the best learning environments operate at the nexus of the principles associated with learner-, assessment-, and knowledge-centered classrooms. For example, the feedback advocated by assessment-centered classrooms directly influences learners and their abilities to reflect on their developing understanding. The knowledge and standards used to design instruction have a direct impact on the activities used to help students construct knowledge. Finally, the standards chosen to guide instruction should closely align with the evaluations used to assess student understanding. The ideas behind *How People Learn* and *How People Learn II* show that a holistic approach is necessary to adequately accommodate the intricacies of learning.

Figure 1.1. *Components and Their Attributes of How Students Learn Best*

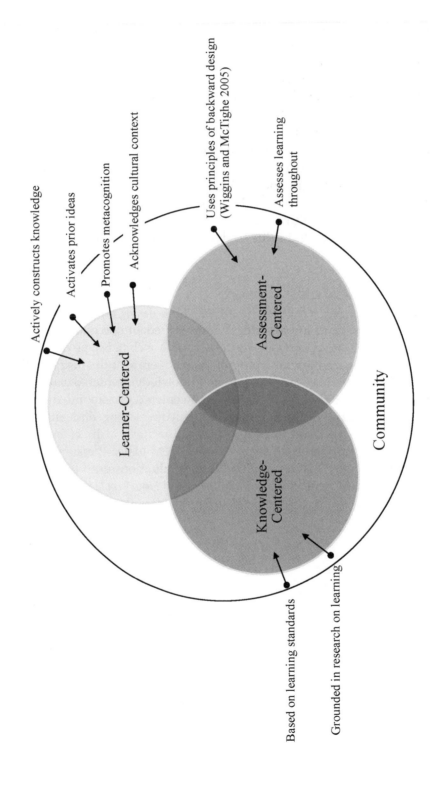

Actively constructs knowledge

Activates prior ideas

Promotes metacognition

Acknowledges cultural context

Uses principles of backward design (Wiggins and McTighe 2005)

Assesses learning throughout

Learner-Centered

Assessment-Centered

Knowledge-Centered

Community

Based on learning standards

Grounded in research on learning

Note: The combination of learner-, knowledge-, and assessment-centeredness creates a classroom community that is based on how students learn best.

Sources: Bransford, Brown, and Cocking (2000); NAESM (2018).

Conclusions

All of these developments in the study of learning have led to a new understanding of teaching and why instructional sequence matters for learners. As I have illustrated above, new theories about why instructional sequence matters are coming into focus. Before school even begins, young children already know a surprising amount about the world they live in and have innate intellectual characteristics similar to scientists and statisticians. They know basic principles in many different science disciplines (physical science, life science, and Earth and space science) as well as the beginnings of valid and reliable ways to generate knowledge (using scientific practices). If students bring to school instinctive inquiry skills that they use to learn about their world, their teachers can capitalize on what the students know and are able to do as a starting point for instruction. In addition, if students prune out weak knowledge structures so the strong ones can flourish, their teachers must focus instruction on activities where students' firsthand experiences with data and evidence help them construct sound conceptual understanding. Finally, supportive environments nurture, build, and sustain students' thinking abilities so they can transfer knowledge to new situations. Students do not come to school a blank slate ready to be inscribed with knowledge, but rather they have ideas about science and the practices used to generate reliable and valid knowledge.

If students develop their abilities to understand and use science practices, they can ask better questions, design more appropriate ways to seek answers to their questions, and collect more dependable sources of data and evidence. Supportive education environments should consider the implications of cognition and learning when developing instructional practices. *Explore-before-explain* teaching focuses on using developmental psychology, neuroscience, and cognitive science research and is all about using simple shifts in instructional sequence to far better orchestrate learning for students.

Activity Box:
Thinking About Early Science Learning

Reflect on an experience with young children in which they might have constructed knowledge about their surroundings from firsthand experiences. Code the knowledge-building strategies they used (critical thinking, scientific reasoning, pattern recognition, etc.) and any science discipline they may have learned about (physical, life, Earth, and space).

Summary Questions:

1. Explain how can the way you design a lesson reflect both the nature of science and what we know about how people learn.

2. How does this align with the way you think you would design your science lessons?

Connecting Hands-On With Minds-On Experiences

Chapter 2

Learning about learning is an important task associated with becoming an *explore-before-explain* teacher. While young children might have natural inquisitiveness and sophisticated reasoning abilities, you may wonder whether it is necessary to create learning environments where students construct all scientific knowledge on their own. Again, to be clear, *explore-before-explain* teaching is not about students constructing all science knowledge from firsthand experiences alone. A solely discovery-based approach to all learning is not optimal for a variety of reasons.

First, some science concepts are inaccessible through the types of hands-on experiences students encounter in typical classroom settings. Second, many concepts that took hundreds of years for scientists to invent are needless for students to construct on their own. Science knowledge would not have progressed as rapidly if the point of education were to have students construct ideas all on their own without building on the knowledge base. Finally, research shows that explaining ideas through lectures, discussions, and readings (authoritative didactic approaches) plays an essential role in learning if students have a framework from which to assimilate new ideas (Duschl, Schweingruber, and Shouse 2007). The point here is not to debate the merits of a discovery versus didactic approach to teaching, but rather to show that both approaches, when used appropriately, enhance learning.

We want students to develop understanding by building on prior experiences. There will be times when a hands-on experience is the best way for students to build knowledge. Other times, lectures, discussions, and readings are the optimal ways to further shape and elaborate student understanding. *Explore-before-explain* teaching recognizes that children are always ready to learn a concept at some level. Although a great deal of children's learning is self-motivated, other people, especially teachers, play a significant role in fostering their intellectual development, and you can do this by creating learner-, knowledge-, and assessment-centered classrooms. Thus, *explore-before-explain* teaching emphasizes that explanations are essential and necessary but should be contextualized by students' firsthand experiences.

In particular, understanding the purpose of explorations and explanations is dictated by the role that the phase plays in learning (Koch 2018). You may think that students, groups, and entire classes cannot think abstractly (I hear this from time to time from teachers at all levels, from elementary through high school). However, in my experience, thinking abstractly is difficult because teachers ask students to reason at a sophisticated level that is disconnected from firsthand experiences. Sometimes we ask students to think abstractly about science without giving them the chance to construct knowledge over time and without direct exposure to phenomena and evidence. For example, occasionally we offer kids new, complex ideas through lectures and discussions without their having had experiences with data and evidence (i.e., disconnected abstraction).

Similarly, we might have students conduct hands-on learning without having them form evidence-based claims supported by credible explanations (e.g., lectures, readings, and discussions). In other words, we ask kids to discover ideas through a hands-on investigation without teacher assistance (i.e., a difficult and unnecessary abstraction). Both explorations and explanations, in combination, are essential for helping students develop rich knowledge structures that promote their abilities to transfer ideas in new settings.

You can cultivate students' inherent inquisitiveness by tapping into their natural curiosity, considering the logic behind their thinking, and then orchestrating activities to scaffold student learning. In this way, you can help students build on what they already know, further grow underdeveloped ideas, and begin to have experiences that allow them to correct inaccurate ideas. An amazing thing happens in students' brains when they construct knowledge based on firsthand experiences: Their experiences link closely to their familiarities with data and evidence. In other words, students' conceptual understanding of science is wired in their brains directly to their immediate experiences.

Common Hands-On Science Instructional Sequences

A significant theme that shows up throughout this book is that students have a high capacity to think logically about science if they have firsthand experiences with phenomena, are encouraged to make claims based on evidence, and have dependable explanations from teachers or other reliable sources. This is the crux of *explore-before-explain* teaching. Thus, the key to planning is to create supportive classroom conditions that foster students' critical thinking about their immediate experiences with science phenomena. Because direct experiences are so crucial in forming a more accurate scientific understanding, they are worth further exploration when we consider hands-on, minds-on science.

Do all hands-on approaches yield the same results? Simply put, the answer is no. Not all hands-on approaches to teaching science intentionally build students' conceptual coherence from a cognitive standpoint (Michaels, Shouse, and Schweingruber 2008). The implications of students' prior science knowledge, and in particular misconceptions, play a pivotal role in learning. Beginning in the early 1980s, conceptual change theory described the importance of prior knowledge and misconceptions and the implications for learning science (Posner et al. 1982). Student ideas (including misconceptions) are the basis for helping students understand, test, refine, and reformulate conceptions based on data and evidence. Misconceptions are important from a cognitive standpoint, because only if students find new ideas more compelling do they change and begin to revise their initial conceptions and create new theories about how the world works.

A strength in a well-designed, hands-on sequence of instruction is the ability to promote conceptual change, because ideas stimulated at the onset of instruction can be tested and investigated through hands-on, minds-on experiences. Data and evidence from experiences become the basis for students' explanations of science. In this view, effective learning activities, and lesson planning, require a purposeful interaction between students' prior knowledge and thinking about their immediate experiences

Chapter 2

to construct accurate understanding. Research on students' misconceptions supports this assertion and has shown that teaching is likely to be ineffective unless it takes learners' perspectives into account (Driver et al. 1994). I cannot emphasize enough the importance of students' prior knowledge and evidenced-based experiences in science learning at the onset of new units of study.

Common hands-on instructional sequences in classrooms can be divided into two broad categories: (1) the traditional hands-on approach, when teachers provide explanations before experiences; and (2) the learning cycle, when teachers provide experiences before explanations.

The Traditional Hands-On Approach

The traditional hands-on science education sequence divides instruction into three phases of instruction: (1) inform, (2) verify, and (3) practice (Abraham 1992). In the first phase, students are informed about what they are to know. Lectures or textbook readings are ways to inform students about specific scientific ideas. Next, students verify new knowledge learned from lectures and readings through laboratory activities or demonstrations by which they can confirm concepts, theories, and facts with data. Finally, students answer questions or work problems to practice their new knowledge in other circumstances. Using a traditional hands-on sequence gives teachers the task of identifying major science concepts and presenting them in clear ways to students. Once the students learn new ideas, they practice them in a range of situations. Although evidence should always play a role in learning, data and students' immediate experiences are not at the heart of the traditional hands-on sequence. Rather, the teacher's explanation plays a central role in learning, and data support ideas that have been constructed firsthand by students.

The Learning Cycle

Conversely, *explore-before-explain* instructional sequences place the experience first and the explanation second. *Explore-before-explain* sequences can be traced back to the Science Curriculum Improvement Study learning cycle, a curriculum divided into three phases: (1) exploration, (2) invention (concept introduction), and (3) discovery (concept application) (Karplus and Their 1967). The exploration phase is a time to make students' ideas explicit. Teachers provide firsthand experiences for students to investigate through laboratory experiences or demonstrations that allow students to collect data. The exploration phase focuses on explorations of content and not procedural tasks (e.g., learning how to use a microscope, how to use a pipette, how to use a scale or balance). Collecting data is central to science instruction because experiences provide the basis to build deeper conceptual understanding. Next, the concept introduction phase derives concepts and new terminology from the data (Abraham 1992). This is a time for students to explain their ideas and to present new ideas that they cannot invent on their own and that have already been provided. Finally, the application phase allows students to elaborate on and verify their new knowledge in other contexts. The application phase is a chance for students to explore the usefulness of new ideas in other circumstances.

The Importance of Sequencing Hands-On With Minds-On

Although investigatory experiences can inherently be engaging for students due to their hands-on nature, in order for the experience to be minds-on, these experiences must integrate with the flow of instruction. Unfortunately, the research on laboratory experiences has revealed that too often when the hands-on part of science is disconnected from content, students leave with a false understanding of the nature of science and view content as separate from practice (Singer, Hilton, and Schweingruber 2006). This same line of research has even shown that labs, when not integrated into the flow of classroom instruction, are no more effective than other instructional approaches used in a similar isolated fashion (e.g., lectures, discussions, and readings on their own; Singer, Hilton, and Schweingruber 2006). For example, merely doing a hands-on lab for activity's sake may interest students but not allow them to form an evidence-based claim.

Similarly, students may be intellectually engaged in a stimulating teacher lecture but may also not have firsthand experiences that allow them to construct knowledge. Debating the use of an isolated approach is not the point here. Whatever the mode of instruction, the research suggests that students need multiple different exposures, and these exposures must be tied to the students' prior knowledge and framed in a relevant context (Banilower et al. 2010; Bransford, Brown, and Cocking 2000). Thus, how we sequence science instruction plays a vital role in helping novices learn science.

The critical aspect of the learning cycle is that students have the chance to collect data and investigate science before being introduced to new terminologies and concepts. In the learning cycle, students use their prior experiences and data gathered in the exploration phase to formulate scientific ideas in the concept introduction phase. The learning cycle allows students to generalize concepts and theories from data collected during laboratory experiences or other direct observations of phenomena and have those ideas backed up with authoritative explanations.

The learning cycle also allows teachers to introduce facts, terms, and concepts in a very meaningful way and helps students invent accurate scientific understanding rather than trying to discover science ideas all on their own (Abraham 1992; Atkin and Karplus 1962; Brown and Abell 2007a). Discrete facts and science vocabulary are directly linked to the scientific ideas students have built through their explorations. National standards do not deny that facts are essential for thinking and developing understanding. However, the research shows that knowing a list of disconnected facts does not equal usable knowledge. Usable science knowledge connects and organizes facts around essential concepts. Organizing facts around important concepts supports understanding for transfer to other contexts rather than only remembering ideas. Here is why authoritative explanations (e.g., teacher lectures, readings, and discussions) can be particularly potent learning experiences for students. A teacher's explanation provides new ideas, terms, and concepts directly tied to students' immediate experiences and knowledge that they have created firsthand. As a result, students develop the ability to use scientific vocabulary correctly, appropriately, and situated in context.

Research on expertise demonstrates that an expert's ability to solve problems relies on a rich body of knowledge that is interconnected and usable (Bransford, Brown, and Cocking 2000). A common misconception regarding the learning cycle is that teachers should never tell students anything directly, when in fact, teaching by telling is very impactful if students have a meaningful perspective in which to frame new knowledge.

Just think about the powerful effects of the learning cycle from a developmental, neurological, cognitive, and conceptual change standpoint: The advancement of students' science understanding is based on the knowledge they have constructed and the practices they used to formulate new ideas. Their firsthand experiences contextualize additional supporting knowledge and deeper conceptual understanding. Thus, in students' brains, neural connections are created, fine-tuned, and strengthened based on their immediate experiences.

In a traditional hands-on sequence, students learn concepts, theories, and facts in the first phase of instruction. Then, they generalize these new ideas to their data. This approach is counterproductive for many reasons. First, if teachers start lessons by telling or giving students information, through lectures or textbook readings, those students are denied the opportunity to show what they already know and to challenge themselves to make sense of scientific phenomena intellectually.

Second, teaching content first and providing experiences afterward fails to link specific content with important science processes, giving students a false image of science. Reliable data-producing experiences generate valid and accurate scientific knowledge.

Third, from a cognitive angle, students construct the link between provided ideas and experiences and data aimed to verify knowledge. Although students still construct understanding, the learning processes are associated with students attaching meaning to what they carry out through experiments.

Finally, learning by listening is valid only if one considers something straightforward such as "red light means stop" and "green light means go." Developing a deep conceptual understanding, including scientific thinking, requires a multitude of well-orchestrated activities that must come before telling students new ideas. The evidence is quite clear that students learn less when they passively listen and have little context in which to conceptualize new ideas (Bransford, Brown, and Cocking 2000).

Forming a Theoretical Framework for Science Teaching

Science instruction is best carried out with intentionality. A theoretical framework for how you design your lessons—that is, your mind-set—should be informed by current research and allow for rigorous investigation through empirical testing in real-life daily classroom settings. Being clear up front about what the most optimal learning looks like is the first step in becoming an *explore-before-explain* teacher. Always keep in mind the importance of exploratory experiences providing the foundation for all future learning. Using an *explore-before-explain* mind-set as the backbone for daily lessons, long-term curriculum planning, and goal setting within professional learning communities can be a powerful way to transform learning and cultivate in students the skills necessary to be successful in school and science.

Activity Box:
Maximizing the Impact
of Hands-On Teaching

1. After reading the "Common Hands-On Science Instructional Sequences" section in Chapter 2, make a bulleted list of the pros and cons of using a learning cycle compared with a traditional hands-on approach.

2. Add any additional pros or cons to your list based on your firsthand experiences with children.

3. Post your list in your planner, on your desk, or on your computer so you can reflect on it frequently when designing lessons.

Chapter 3

Modern Sequences of Instruction

Chapter 3

Sequencing science instruction in *explore-before-explain* arrangements is a research-based way of understanding how students learn science best. Two popular contemporary approaches that promote explorations before explanations are the POE (Predict, Observe, and Explain) and 5E (Engage, Explore, Explain, Elaborate, Evaluate) instructional models. With both models, it is important that the phases be linked to the research on cognition, the role of prior knowledge, and the learning cycle. Although both models use *explore-before-explain* sequences, they are not the same approach. The POE Model is a 1- to 2-day lesson approach that can be used to build toward more extensive 5E sequences of science instruction (5- to 10-day approach). Both instructional designs are beneficial for creating more learner-centered environments by tapping into students' prior knowledge and encouraging critical thinking. Both models can help facilitate *explore-before-explain* teaching. One main difference is that the POE Model offers us an instructional practice for using demonstration in science:

Predict → Observe → Explain.

While the 5E Model does not offer a specific instructional practice like the POE does, it provides us guidance on the necessary sequence in our instructional practices that is deeply connected to cognitive science research and an advancement over the learning cycle:

Engage → Explore → Explain → Elaborate → Evaluate.

Let's look more closely at the details of the POE and 5E models.

The POE (Predict, Observe, and Explain) Model

The POE Model is a student-centered sequence for engaging students' ideas in one- to two-day lessons during science demonstrations and labs (Haysom and Bowen 2010; Stepans 1996). This model emphasizes explanations based on data and observations, and it can include many opportunities for formative and summative assessments and extensions to other situations. The phases of the POE sequence parallel the exploration and concept introduction phases of the Science Curriculum Improvement Study (SCIS) learning cycle and can be used for creating more extensive 5E units.

The Predict stage engages students' interest in the lesson and identifies their initial conceptions (including misconceptions). Activities stimulate student ideas and focus learning on specific topics.

Next, the Observe stage presents students with firsthand experiences with quantitative or qualitative observations, data, or other evidence. During the Observe stage, activities are performed and data are collected.

Finally, the Explain stage allows students to generate scientifically accurate ideas based on data they have collected or observed during the demonstration. Help students by guiding them in how to think about the activity (e.g., "What patterns did you notice?" or "Were there any cause-and-effect relationships?"), so they can make evidence-based claims. Only after students have explained the phenomena in their own way should you try introducing new terms and concepts.

The 5E Instructional Model

The 5E Instructional Model includes the following phases: Engage, Explore, Explain, Elaborate, and Evaluate (Bybee 1997). The beginning and ending phases (i.e., Engage and Evaluate) are new additions to the learning cycle based on advances in cognitive science research (Brown and Abell 2007b). The remaining three phases—Explore, Explain, and Elaborate—retain some features of the SCIS learning cycle but have been modified based on advances in learning theory. Formative feedback cuts across all phases of the 5E Instructional Model and provides a gauge of student understanding. In addition, formative assessments promote students' thinking and reflection on their knowledge and learning.

Chapter 3

Engage

During the Engage phase, you provide meaningful and relevant science activities to capture students' interest in learning (Bybee 2002). This phase also evaluates students' prior knowledge and experiences (remember the importance of promoting conceptual change). During this time, have discussions, motivate student learning, and focus the lesson on learning targets. Similar to scientists, who are inquisitive and interested in how the natural world works, students should be intrigued by the learning activities during the Engage phase. Ask open-ended questions that are closely connected to the content to spark student thinking as well as ones that may encourage students to raise questions of their own. Avoid introducing new science terminology because students have no frame of reference yet to make meaningful links between new content and prior experiences.

During the Engage activities, check students' understanding and collect their ideas, including misconceptions. Twenty unique students rarely bring 20 different conceptions of the phenomena explored during engagement activities. Students' preconceptions can be grouped together if there are only a few varying conceptions across the class. Eliciting students' thoughts is valuable regardless of the correctness of their ideas. When we elicit students' ideas at the beginning of instruction, it primes their brains for what they will be learning about in the unit of study. The more students connect new ideas with their existing knowledge, the better they will understand that new knowledge.

Explore

The Explore phase affords opportunities for students to conduct hands-on and minds-on activities. Students explore new science ideas and collect either quantitative or qualitative data. First and foremost, carefully choose demonstrations or laboratory activities and other experiences based on the content learned. Offer directions on how students will perform exploration; however, focus on the procedural aspects, safety, and collaboration (whether the activity is individual or done in groups) associated with the investigation versus explaining content.

During this time, students should focus on data collection and beginning analysis. In addition, they should be open-minded and willing to change ideas as they explore because they may have evidence that contradicts their initial ideas. Because scientists work collaboratively, many exploration activities also include opportunities to cooperate with others and advance group thinking. In the Explore phase, students are not responsible for looking to outside sources for content knowledge or checking science research to endorse or disconfirm their main findings.

Explain

In the Explain phase, students draw on the Engage and Explore activities to construct explanations based on evidence of the phenomena. In other words, the Explain phase is directly linked to exploration and engagement activities. Students should look for patterns in data, decipher important relationships, and use scientific reasoning to explain ideas on a conceptual level. At this point, the students do not look for additional data through reference materials or other hands-on activities to validate their ideas. They should explain their understanding of the science investigated so far based on the data they have collected and analyzed.

Teachers should introduce language unique to science and different forms of representations (e.g., analogies, diagrams, formulas) to increase student understanding. Using readings during the Explain phase can be particularly effective for learning because students will then have a framework for incorporating new knowledge. This process of providing scientific terminology and new representations helps students incorporate new terminology in a meaningful framework of understanding and use new terms correctly in future circumstances. Also, teachers should supply supporting content not easily discoverable or accessible from hands-on investigations. When you provide the concepts after students have had a chance to formulate evidence-based claims, they restructure, reshape, and refine their prior conceptions. Explanations should focus on content very closely related to explorations.

Teachers should also offer practice activities for the new terms they have provided at this potent time for learners. During the Explain phase, practice-type activities help students solidify their understanding of new terms and concepts. Try not to provide all of the intended information for a particular subject unless the ideas are directly associated with explorations that have occurred so far.

Elaborate

In the Elaborate phase, students connect their experiences from the Engage, Explore, and Explain phases to test and verify new understandings in other contexts. The students test out new ideas to see if they work in different settings. The Elaborate phase helps form a more thorough understanding because the activities help validate and extend student knowledge and offer opportunities to practice new terminologies. The teacher should provide activities that help students build on their knowledge to establish a deeper and broader understanding. This is not a chance simply to offer the rest of the ideas important to the unit of study (i.e., to lecture or discuss remaining related content).

Elaborations are doing and thinking based, meaning that students are involved in building, extending, and practicing ideas in novel situations. Elaborations allow students to determine whether ideas are generalizable and whether basic principles and ideas stand true in different contexts. Sometimes, students engage in discussions, Socratic seminars, and other types of argumentative exchanges about the validity and reliability of ideas. This is not a time to elaborate on the content in a trivial sense of the word and learn unrelated science content.

Evaluate

The Evaluate phase is an opportunity for students to reflect on their new conceptions of science and for teachers to evaluate the accuracy of student ideas and what students have learned. Students should think about what they have learned and how far they have come intellectually—that is, engage in *metacognition*, which has a significant effect on learning (see Hattie 2009).

The Evaluate phase allows us to assess whether students have developed knowledge (i.e., whether students' ideas have changed since the Engage phase and whether they have gained new, more sophisticated understanding). Although the Evaluate phase may provide a summative assessment of student knowledge and learning, it is not a chance to reteach content. Use the evaluation activities as a diagnostic tool to decide what content and investigation to introduce next and how.

Conclusions

Both the POE and 5E models sequence science instruction so that students have exploratory opportunities with data and evidence that allow them to generate a scientific claim. Students construct knowledge based on their direct encounters with science phenomena. The connection between the 5Es and the SCIS learning cycle has been the theme of sections in science teaching methods books (see Contant et al. 2018), and research has proven the benefits of the approach for increasing students' motivation and achievement (see Bybee et al. 2006). The popularity of 5E teaching is such that other approaches have been invented that retain the *explore-before-explain* emphasis. For instance, the 7E Model adds phases (i.e., Elicit and Extend) based on cognitive research (Eisenkraft 2003). The Elicit phase occurs at the onset of a new lesson to ensure that teachers stimulate student ideas and assess prior knowledge. In the Extend phase, teachers have students transfer knowledge to new and different circumstances. In addition, teachers can easily promote more purposeful collaboration in the POE Model by adding a Share phase ("PSOE"), where students talk through their ideas before observing and collecting data.

There is so much compelling support for learning cycle sequences that scholars have suggested the approach as a central theory of instruction (Bybee 1997). Because so many of your professional experiences will involve personal reflection, this is a good time to look inward. I hope that you are beginning to discover the power of *explore-before-explain* approaches for learners. Before we jump in and design *explore-before-explain* sequences of instruction, let's make one more connection and strengthen your knowledge base for science teaching with *A Framework for K–12 Science Education* (National Research Council 2012) and the *Next Generation Science Standards* (NGSS Lead States 2013).

Activity Box:
Inventorying Science Practices

1. After reading Chapter 3, make a list of hands-on activities that you have recently used over the past grading period.

2. Categorize your list of hands-on activities according to whether they might fit in a POE Model or a 5E instructional sequence.

3. Discuss with members of your professional learning community or science team where you might be able to use common POE and 5E practices in your curriculum that best meet student needs in your district.

Chapter 4

Content and Process Working Together

Chapter 4

The POE (Predict, Observe, and Explain) and 5E (Engage, Explore, Explain, Elaborate, Evaluate) instructional models help clarify when and how we teach, and *A Framework for K–12 Science Education* (*Framework*; National Research Council [NRC] 2012) helps identify what we should consider teaching to achieve higher levels of scientific literacy for our students. The integration of science and engineering practices, crosscutting concepts, and disciplinary core content is known as three-dimensional learning and is critical to promoting science literacy. Three-dimensional learning advocates are moving lessons away from presenting isolated facts toward having students use logical reasoning and science practices to show knowledge in use (Krajcik et al. 2014). As noted in *Taking Science to School*,

> *The learning and instruction research suggests a dramatic departure from this typical approach, revealing that science instruction can be much more powerful and can take on new forms that enable students to participate in science as practice and to master core conceptual domains more fully.* (Duschl, Schweingruber, and Shouse 2007, p. 254)

Let's look more closely at the three dimensions of knowledge and abilities so we can fuse them together when we teach.

Dimension 1: Science and Engineering Practices

Students must directly experience and be explicitly taught the practices of science to gain deep understanding, reinforcing the need for classroom activities that involve students in investigations. The essential science and engineering practices (SEPs) require students to mesh skills such as observation, inference, investigation, and problem solving to develop new content ideas (Bybee 2012). The *Framework* identifies eight SEPs (shown in bold below) that are essential in a K–12 science and engineering curriculum and are taught just as one would teach content (NRC 2012). The eight practices embody the multifaceted, overlapping processes that scientists use to develop and share knowledge about the natural world and are as follows:

1. A basic component of an investigation is **asking questions and defining problems** that can be answered using observation, data collection, and empirical tests.

2. Understanding science may necessitate **developing and using models,** either physical or conceptual, to help explain and make predictions about phenomena.

3. A major part of science is **planning and carrying out investigations** that may require defining variables, identifying data sources, and planning procedures to yield accurate evidence-based claims.

4. After investigating and observing phenomena, scientists must engage in **analyzing and interpreting data** to explore any potential cause-and-effect relationships and to notice patterns in the data.

5. In science, **using mathematical, informational, and computer technology** and **computational thinking** are tools to help represent and make sense of physical information.

6. The main goal of science is **constructing explanations** for scientific phenomena based on data and evidence. In engineering, a main goal is developing a **design solution** in response to a problem.

7. Scientists rationalize the strengths and weaknesses of their explanations based on data and evidence. **Engaging in argument from evidence** is a way for scientists to offer the best, most unbiased explanation possible.

8. Science advances by building on the existing knowledge base. **Obtaining, evaluating, and communicating information** is essential for filling gaps in our understanding.

Each practice can range from student directed to teacher directed, allowing for a whole host of implementation strategies. For example, consider the first essential practice (asking questions and defining problems). If students have prerequisite experiences with content and practices, they can generate testable questions and define problems on their own or in groups. However, students often benefit from more guidance and need to learn how to ask testable questions and define problems. Keep in mind that the research has shown that children's ability to reason related to performing experiments and answering scientific questions can be advanced with effective instruction and supporting environments (Donovan and Bransford 2005; Duschl, Schweingruber, and Shouse 2007).

All of the essential practices can be self-directed by students or directed by teachers to learn the content. The practices are overlapping, meaning that asking questions leads to designing and conducting experiments and then to making sense of observations derived from experiences with data and evidence. In addition, all of the practices build on each other over time (see Appendix F of the *Next Generation Science Standards* [*NGSS*] for the essential elements and the SEP learning progressions; NGSS Lead States 2013). Thus, wedding the SEPs with the content is a way to integrate the hands-on part of science with content (Singer, Hilton, and Schweingruber 2006).

Dimension 2: Crosscutting Concepts

The crosscutting concepts (CCs) provide an organizational framework for helping students connect knowledge from different disciplines. The *Framework* identifies seven CCs that span across disciplinary boundaries (Duschl 2012). The CCs help students deepen their understanding because they emphasize students leading the knowledge-building process by doing science (NRC 2012).

Chapter 4

Scientists often use CCs without coding them as science. Every day, scientists look for patterns and cause-and-effect relationships (both CCs) by analyzing and interpreting data (SEPs). However, students who are novice science learners benefit from explicit instruction on the CCs.

Brief examples of the seven CCs (shown in bold) and closely related practices (shown in italics) are as follows:

1. During empirical investigations, noticing **patterns** in data is often an initial step in organizing phenomena, constructing inferences, and asking scientific questions. Looking for patterns is implicit in the essential practice of *analyzing and interpreting data* (NRC 2012).

2. Sometimes a major goal of science investigations is to investigate the causal relationship between variables in a situation. Investigating **cause and effect** provides an understanding of the phenomena that enable accurate predictions and logical reasoning. Cause-and-effect relationships are closely tied to the essential practice of *planning and carrying out investigations* (NRC 2012).

3. When exploring some science topics, scientists must consider the **scale, proportion, and quantity** used to measure the magnitude of the phenomena under study. An understanding of scale and quantity requires a scientist to use the appropriate measures necessary for understanding the system. Proportional thinking in science helps explain the relationship between factors from a mathematical perspective.

4. To break down a complicated phenomenon into a more simplified and understandable form, scientists often think in terms of **systems and system models** to examine a specific feature of the natural world. Scrutinizing a system and system models (both physical and conceptual models) allows scientists to focus on some aspect of a phenomenon to understand the interactions that occur among factors. A well-understood system or model both explains science phenomena and allows for making accurate predictions.

5. Understanding how **energy and matter** transfer and are conserved is important for knowing the "inputs, outputs and flows or transfers within a system" (NRC 2012, p. 95). The law of conservation allows scientists to analyze how matter and energy transfer to better understand a system of study.

6. Many science phenomena can be understood best as complementary properties. Thinking about some science topics through **structure and function** analysis allows scientists to understand key relationships among parts of the system under study.

7. A system can be steady or react to changes that influence the interconnections among variables in the system. Examining the system through a **stability and change** perspective allows scientists to understand the disturbances influencing the system being explored.

Using Observe and Explore activities near the onset of lessons, as advocated by the POE and 5E models, allows us to easily target CCs that may help students bridge databased experiences and specific science claims. Similarly to the SEPs, how students make use of the CCs depends on their experience and knowledge. Students may be able to look for patterns and cause-and-effect relationships in data with little guidance. Conversely, teachers may need to use probing questions and be explicit in helping students explore conversions and transformations or the structure and function of a system of study. All of the CCs build on each other over time (see Appendix G of the *NGSS* for the essential elements and the SEP learning progressions; NGSS Lead States 2013).

Finally, once again, research has shown that even very young children can identify patterns and cause-and-effect relationships in supportive environments where they have direct experiences with data and evidence (Donovan and Bransford 2005; Duschl, Schweingruber, and Shouse 2007).

Dimension 3: Disciplinary Core Ideas

The disciplinary core ideas (DCIs) include descriptions and explanations of natural phenomena. Third- through fifth-grade science is organized around four core areas that focus on ideas central to developing science understanding: physical science (PS); life science (LS); Earth and space science (ESS); and engineering, technology, and applications of science (ET) (NRC 2012; see Table 4.1, p. 32). The DCIs are not an exhaustive explanation of the science under study. Rather, they are central to explaining a host of phenomena to help students better understand how the world works. Each core area has supporting component ideas that should guide the types of explorations that teachers use with students.

Chapter 4

Table 4.1. *Disciplinary Core Ideas for Grades 3–5*

Grade 3
• 3-PS2: Motion and Stability: Forces and Interactions
• 3-LS1: From Molecules to Organisms: Structures and Processes
• 3-LS2: Ecosystems: Interactions, Energy, and Dynamics
• 3-LS3: Heredity: Inheritance and Variation of Traits
• 3-LS4: Biological Evolution: Unity and Diversity
• 3-ESS2: Earth's Systems
• 3-ESS3: Earth and Human Activity
Grade 4
• 4-PS3: Energy
• 4-PS4: Waves and Their Applications in Technologies for Information Transfer
• 4-LS1: From Molecules to Organisms: Structures and Processes
• 4-ESS1: Earth's Place in the Universe
• 4-ESS2: Earth's Systems
• 4-ESS3: Earth and Human Activity
Grade 5
• 5-PS1: Matter and Its Interactions
• 5-PS2: Motion and Stability: Forces and Interactions
• 5-PS3: Energy
• 5-LS1: From Molecules to Organisms: Structures and Processes
• 5-LS2: Ecosystems: Interactions, Energy, and Dynamics
• 5-ESS1: Earth's Place in the Universe
• 5-ESS2: Earth's Systems
• 5-ESS3: Earth and Human Activity
• 3-5-ETS1: Engineering Design

The full supporting component idea statements are available online (see *www.next-genscience.org/sites/default/files/AllDCI.pdf*; NGSS Lead States 2013).

Taken as a whole, the DCIs introduce students to many important aspects of physical science while developing a clearer idea of essential content expectations. Each DCI is most effectively taught when intertwined with an SEP and a CC.

Content and Process Working Together

Performance Expectations

The *NGSS* blends DCIs, SEPs, and CCs to form performance expectations (PEs). If you are using complex standards such as the *NGSS* to guide your curriculum, you may need to deconstruct the standards into smaller chunks of information pertinent for scaffolding learning. Krajcik and colleagues (2014) have provided a 10-step developmental process to design lessons to address the *NGSS*.

PEs have been conceptualized as analogous to a rope, wherein the three dimensions are similar to threads that have been woven or braided together into a larger and stronger form (NGSS Lead States 2013). The three dimensions (i.e., DCIs, SEPs, and CCs) represent the threads, whereas the PEs are the resulting combined intertwined fibers. Thus, the PEs represent an amalgamation of knowledge that is more robust than the representative parts. The PEs also include clarification and assessment boundary statements that offer examples and identify the breadth of knowledge encompassed by the statement. In short, PEs represent what it means to be proficient in science and illustrate goals for higher levels of scientific literacy. The PEs provide guidance on the knowledge in practice that students should have once they have finished a course of study. For instance, consider the following PE, which states,

> **Plan and conduct an investigation to provide evidence of the effects of balanced and unbalanced forces on the motion of an object.** *[Clarification Statement: Examples could include an unbalanced force on one side of a ball can make it start moving; and, balanced forces pushing on a box from both sides will not produce any motion at all.] [Assessment Boundary: Assessment is limited to one variable at a time: number, size, or direction of forces. Assessment does not include quantitative force size, only qualitative and relative. Assessment is limited to gravity being addressed as a force that pulls objects down.]* (NGSS Lead States 2013, 3-PS2-1)

Working backward, we can unwrap the components of the PE. The PE explicitly identifies the science and engineering practices of conducting an investigation when investigating science phenomena related to the influence of balanced and unbalanced forces on the motion of an object. Included in the PE are the DCIs necessary to gain proficiency. The DCIs state that students should know the characteristics used to describe forces and how they interact to create motion:

> *Each force acts on one particular object and has both strength and a direction. An object at rest typically has multiple forces acting on it, but they add to give zero net force on the object. Forces that do not sum to zero can cause changes in the object's speed or direction of motion. (Boundary: Qualitative and conceptual, but not quantitative addition of forces are used at this level.)* (NGSS Lead States 2013, PS2.A)

Implicit in the SEPs of conducting an investigation related to the content is the crosscutting concept of cause and effect. Students should be able to explain what happens

Chapter 4

in terms of the inputs and outputs when objects with different forces interact on an object.

Some PEs lend themselves to direct translation into classroom practices; however, others benefit from being broken down into smaller learning objectives that form the scaffolding for the overall attainment of the PE. PEs represent end goals and not single-day learning objectives. Many teachers have success creating lesson-level PEs that include all three dimensions of the *Framework* and act as stepping-stones toward mastering more sophisticated PEs (see Krajcik et al. 2014). In addition, many teachers bundle together PEs so students move seamlessly from one topic to another while gaining more elaborate understandings. By always keeping PEs in mind in your planning, you can create more rigorous and meaningful science learning experiences.

Science and Practice: Doing and Learning Together

When teachers know the destination, they can design enabler activities in specific phases to ensure that students obtain specific learning objectives related to the topic studied. An *explore-before-explain* mind-set requires us to move away from memorization and teach in ways that promote deep conceptual understanding. There are numerous possibilities for including SEPs and CCs during all phases of the 5E or POE Model depending on the desired learning outcomes. Students benefit from being explicitly taught SEPs and CCs during the appropriate phase of the 5E (or POE) Model; this knowledge should be cumulatively developed over time. By cultivating a way of thinking about science, we can improve students' abilities to solve problems and become knowledge builders and meaning makers.

Table 4.2 summarizes the dimensions emphasized in each model lesson. Each of the model lessons integrates the three dimensions of the *Framework* to help students think critically, problem solve, and develop understanding. In addition, each model lesson contributes to students developing the knowledge and abilities to succeed at the PEs.

Table 4.2. *Curriculum Grid Identifying NGSS Standards Present in Model Lessons*

Dimension	NGSS dimension	Chapter 6: Thermal Energy	Chapter 7: Invisible Test Tube	Chapter 8: Magnetism	Chapter 9: Circuits	Chapter 10: Gliding	Chapter 11: Is It a Change?	Chapter 12: Ecosystems	Chapter 13: Erosion
SEPs	Asking questions and defining problems	♦		♦	♦	♦	♦	♦	♦
	Analyzing and interpreting data	♦	♦	♦	♦	♦	♦		♦
	Developing and using models	♦	♦			♦		♦	
	Planning and carrying out investigations	♦		♦	♦	♦	♦	♦	♦
	Using mathematics thinking					♦	♦		
	Constructing explanations	♦	♦	♦	♦		♦	♦	♦
	Obtaining, evaluating, and communicating information		♦	♦	♦	♦			
CCs	Patterns		♦	♦	♦	♦	♦		
	Systems and system models	♦	♦						
	Energy and matter	♦			♦				
	Cause and effect						♦		♦
	Scale, proportion, and quantity						♦		

Continued

Table 4.2. (*continued*)

Dimension	NGSS dimension	Chapter 6: Thermal Energy	Chapter 7: Invisible Test Tube	Chapter 8: Magnetism	Chapter 9: Circuits	Chapter 10: Gliding	Chapter 11: Is It a Change?	Chapter 12: Ecosystems	Chapter 13: Erosion
DCIs	PS3.A: Definitions of energy	♦			♦				
	PS3.B: Conservation of energy transfer	♦			♦				
	PS4.B: Electromagnetic radiation		♦						
	PS2.B: Types of interactions			♦					
	PS2.A: Forces and motion					♦			
	PS1.A: Structure and properties of matter						♦		
	PS1.B: Chemical reactions						♦		
	LS2.A: Relationships in ecosystems							♦	
	LS2.B: Cycles of matter and energy							♦	
	LS1.A: Structure and function							♦	
	ESS2.A: Earth materials and systems							♦	♦
	LS4.C: Adaptation								♦
	ESS1.C: The history of planet Earth								♦
	LS4.A: Evidence of common ancestry								♦

Conclusions

Thus far, I have briefly described science understanding and abilities that present practices, logical thinking, and content as integrated. The practice of separating process and content does not align with recent advances in scholarship in cognition. Students come with a broad range of knowledge, reasoning abilities, and understanding as a consequence of their interactions with data and evidence. The developmental literature has shown that although scientific reasoning can be complex, students' capabilities and logical thinking can be advanced by effectively structuring activities and providing supportive environments (Donovan and Bransford 2005; Duschl, Schweingruber, and Shouse 2007). This is a key aspect of the research literature to keep in mind when thinking about students' abilities.

Science standards, lessons, and curricular design should be well conceived, well designed, and well implemented in a coordinated system. By interweaving the hands-on doing with critical thinking and core ideas, we can start to provide a more beneficial learning environment, as called for by *America's Lab Report* (Singer, Hilton, and Schweingruber 2006). Therefore, with the scholarship on cognition and effective integrated instruction in mind, let's look at where to start planning *explore-before-explain* sequences of science instruction.

> ### Activity Box:
> ### Pairing Practices With Crosscutting Concepts
>
> After reading the essential science and engineering practices and crosscutting concepts sections, describe recent hands-on activities that you have had students perform. How do you help them think logically about the data? List the SEPs that students used and their complementary CCs.

Chapter 5

Where to Start

Chapter 5

Tackling your first POE (Predict, Observe, and Explain) or 5E (Engage, Explore, Explain, Elaborate, Evaluate) lesson design may seem like a daunting task. Although this is not a how-to book with systematic instructions, I hope that the first chapters have helped you think about the most effective teaching and learning environments from a more pedagogical perspective. Although there are many ways to start POE and 5E planning, I have found through working with teachers and students that beginning planning with specific phases and outcomes in mind brings greater leverage to the overall lesson, unit, and curriculum design.

First, you can think of components of the phases of instruction as either *destinations* or *enablers*. *Destinations* are where we want students to end up as learners in science classrooms. *Enablers* are activities and phases of instruction necessary to help students reach the desired outcomes. Enablers help provide students with a clear picture of where they are going and equip them with the knowledge and abilities necessary to arrive at the destination. Both destinations and enablers are critical in an effective instructional sequence.

Second, I have built my planning considerations around the principles of how students learn best and their subcomponents. You may find it helpful to go back and forth between the research chapter (Chapter 1, p. 1) and this chapter, and examine the planning considerations with Figure 1.1 (p. 8).

Third, rather than creating something new from scratch, you might reflect on a hands-on teaching experience you've used in the past to see if it can be redesigned to fit the 5E Instructional Model. I have provided six semi-rank-ordered planning considerations that can help teachers construct 5E units. I offer semi-rank-ordered because creating effective 5Es requires simultaneously thinking about other phases of the model. Therefore, while you may place primacy on planning activities for one phase, other related phases should be in your mind. Following the planning considerations are activities I have used in my own practice as well as with preservice teachers and current teachers to design effective 5E units.

Teachers Are Designers

Becoming *explore-before-explain* teachers requires us to think about teaching and learning in new ways. For many, the research and standards alone are not enough to develop an *explore-before-explain* mind-set for teaching. We need to be able to see examples and create experiences that we can test with students. It is not until we use *explore-before-explain* teaching with students that we see the benefits of the approach. Figure 5.1 depicts the two stages of this approach in the simplest form and the corresponding phases of the 5E Instructional Model.

I consider this a two-stage approach because *explore-before-explain* teaching requires us to think in ways that promote the special combination of *Next Generation Science Standards* (*NGSS*) dimensions above the content alone. For students to make an evidence-based claim, they will have to think about the trends, patterns, and relationships between evidence and their observations to make an accurate statement about science.

Figure 5.1. *Two-Stage Approach to Planning Lessons Based on the* NGSS *and Research*

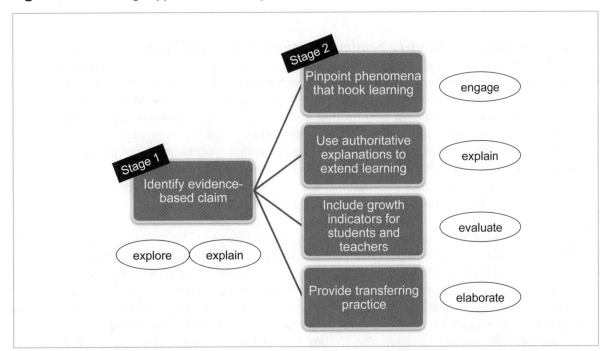

By beginning our focus in design planning on students' evidence-based claims, we promote the importance of science and engineering practices (SEPs) and crosscutting concepts (CCs) in science to the same level as disciplinary core ideas (DCIs).

A two-stage approach acknowledges the necessary conceptual change that many of us go through to be *explore-before-explain* teachers. Only when teachers find new approaches fruitful and plausible and have a chance to test them do they overcome their prior experiences and understandings. We need to get Stage 1 right to move on to the planning considerations in Stage 2. This is all quite logical as you come to understand the philosophy, but it's different from how many of us learned science as students and from the many traditions in schools that use the textbook to drive curricula.

Stage 1

The first stage is planning ways to support students' ongoing development and thinking as they construct a conceptual science framework from their direct experiences with data and evidence. We want students' content understanding to be a direct result of experiences doing science, using the SEPs and CCs. Stage 1 is all about interacting with students as they engage with phenomena to make sense about why something happens or why something works. Students think about data and logically

Chapter 5

interpret what the evidence means about science. Stage 1 includes two main planning considerations.

Consideration 1: Identify Students' Evidence-Based Claims

In Wiggins and McTighe's book *Understanding by Design* (2005), the authors suggested starting to plan with the desired results of teaching and planning activities in mind to best meet the intended learning outcomes. In other words, start lesson design with the end in mind. The student portion that initiates the Explain phase is key because it represents students' construction of conceptual knowledge based on experiences (a significant destination from a learning and cognition standpoint). Students' evidence-based claims represent the knowledge they have constructed and serve as the basis for developing effective teacher explanations and more in-depth investigations.

Starting with the student portion of the Explain phase is also an easy way to develop deeper understanding and make interdisciplinary connections. The sequence of the claims-evidence-reasoning (C-E-R) framework hits many SEPs (e.g., constructing explanations and communicating information) and is a way to encourage students to construct explanations for phenomena during the Explain phase (see McNeill and Krajcik 2012). In addition, the C-E-R framework supports the *Common Core State Standards for English Language Arts*, which suggest that students "provide a conclusion statement or section that follows from and supports the information or explanation presented" (National Governors Association Center for Best Practices and Council of Chief State School Officers 2010). See Table 5.1.

Table 5.1. *Having Students Construct C-E-R Statements*

Claims	Evidence	Reasoning
Students' claims typically represent what they can explain on a conceptual level about science. Normally, I find that the claim is the easiest part for students. When given an investigatory question, and having collected data and evidence, students can construct a claim that addresses the question about specific phenomena. Consequently, it is imperative to have students focus on what the investigatory question is asking..	Evidence represents compelling data that support the claim. One of the key aspects of having students use data to make claims is to think logically about patterns, trends, and any relationships present in the data. Students benefit from thinking about the high and low data points across multiple trials and whether different factors change or remain the same in the investigation.	The reasoning statement is challenging because it requires students to link the evidence with the overarching claim. The reasoning statement explains the underlying scientific principles and links the evidence and the claim. This level of reasoning often requires discussions of appropriate science principles to help explain the claim–evidence link because students are basing the reasoning on their understanding of science content.

Activity Box:
Planning for Student Explanations
During Explain Phase Activities

Driving question for designing student Explain phase activities

- What evidence-based claims can students construct from their data and evidence?

Teacher Planning		Student Tasks	
"Emphasize now"	"Highlight in another phase"	"Emphasize now"	"Highlight in another phase"
• Teach students about the importance of being objective (vs. subjective) in science. • Encourage students to explain in their own words what they have experienced firsthand.	• Explain content before students have a chance to articulate claims. • Provide all of the intended information on the subject.	• Have students articulate their understanding based on data.	• Try to generalize knowledge by testing ideas in other situations.

Consideration 2: Use Explore Activities That Provide Valid and Reliable Data and Can Lead to Accurate Evidence-Based Claims

To get to the Explain phase, students have to have firsthand experiences with data and evidence. Thus, the Explore phase is a significant enabler because it is the basis for the construction of knowledge that is formalized in how students articulate their understanding (evidence-based claims). Many novice students who are learning specific content for the first time benefit from exploration experiences that straightforwardly lead to accurate evidence-based claims. Hands-on activities that do not seamlessly lead to unambiguous evidence-based claims may fit better in other phases (e.g., the Elaborate phase).

The Explore phase is also key in planning because to arrive at a scientific claim, students must "do science." This means that they engage in many SEPs (and possibly CCs) about specific science ideas (DCIs). For instance, they may have had Explore activities that asked them to plan and carry out investigations (SEP). The data gained during their exploration required them to think about patterns, trends, and evidence (SEP). Depending on the nature of the data collected during the exploration, students can engage in mathematical and computational thinking (SEP) and *Common Core State Standards for Mathematics* such as measuring data, numerical calculations, and graphing.

At all of these points in the learning process, students should be aware of the specifics of what they are doing and how science skills allow for the reliable interpretation of data. The result is that students begin to build a complex conceptual understanding of the scientific phenomena because they are organizing their content understanding based on direct encounters with evidence.

Activity Box:
Planning for Exploration Activities

Driving question for the Explore phase activities

- What hands-on, minds-on investigation demonstration will students experience to collect data or evidence?

Teacher Planning		Student Tasks	
"Emphasize now"	"Highlight in another phase"	"Emphasize now"	"Highlight in another phase"
• Carefully select the activity based on the intended learning outcomes. • Offer directions (e.g., how students will work individually or together) and procedures, including safety. • Ask probing questions to prompt student thinking about data.	• Explain content. • Validate the accuracy of data.	• Collect quantitative or qualitative data. • Think logically about trends, patterns, and possible cause-and-effect relationships.	• Endorse or disconfirm main findings with outside sources.

Stage 2

With clearly identified goals for the knowledge that students can construct firsthand, teachers are ready to embark on Stage 2. While this stage is no less important than Stage 1, it does not typically require the same level of conceptual change to develop an *explore-before-explain* mind-set. Several key lesson planning tasks have emerged, and Stage 2 is all about situating learning in a meaningful and relevant context, introducing ideas to promote more sophisticated understanding, and allowing students to test the utility of new knowledge in different circumstances. We can make choices about knowledge assessment probes, teaching methods, resources, materials, and authoritative explanations only after we have decided on the knowledge that students will construct. The logic of the two-stage process applies regardless of content (and discipline). In addition, three different teachers may be working off of the same activity used to help students construct evidence-based claims (Stage 1), but they vary in the specific approaches they use in Stage 2. As designers, we can gain greater curricular coherence if the phenomena, growth factors, explanations, and elaborations we use tie back to the knowledge that students construct from data. Included in Stage 2 are planning considerations 3–6.

Consideration 3: Pinpoint Phenomena That Can Hook Students Into Learning Science

At the beginning of new lessons, teachers have the chance to capture student interest and motivate learning. Identifying a relevant phenomenon that is introduced during the Engage phase is a way to interest students in science and create opportunities to talk about ways to analyze the topic. Simply stated, phenomena are situations that exist and can be observed and whose causes are in question. For instance, students encounter many natural, observable phenomena such as the changing of the seasons and the phases of the Moon. In addition, using project-based situations or social issues to guide the phenomena under study is a research-oriented way to engage students and develop their deep conceptual understanding (Brown and Abell 2008a, 2008b).

Phenomena can look different for students of different ages. Scientific phenomena can range from the complex to the rather simple in scope and are dependent on the learner's background knowledge and experience. With teacher guidance, novice learners can construct accurate claims that explain these phenomena using firsthand experiences with evidence. NSTA Press has many books dedicated to showing how specific phenomena can drive science lessons (Bobrowsky, Korhonen, and Kohtamaki 2014; O'Brien 2010, 2011a, 2011b).

Phenomenon-based teaching is beneficial for both teachers and students. From a teacher's perspective, asking students about a specific phenomenon at the onset of instruction is a way to elicit students' prior knowledge and diagnose what students know and do not know related to the topic (Banilower et al. 2010). In addition, pinpointing a specific phenomenon can create the storyline for your 5Es and show students how different parts of a lesson are connected to an overarching theme. Teachers can use phenomena to drive instruction in narrow to broad topics, and they can use

5Es and POEs to fully or partially address the phenomenon under study. Thus, phenomenon-based teaching allows for a multitude of ways of connecting lessons so they are meaningful for students.

For students, phenomenon-based learning makes science relevant because they believe they are embarking on an exploration of a topic they do not fully understand but that occurs in their daily lives. Phenomenon-based teaching perpetuates curiosity and helps link content to hands-on explorations. For instance, through the collection of quantitative or qualitative data, students arrive at a better understanding of the phenomenon. Once phenomena are chosen to drive learning, students should work alongside teachers to develop SEPs (e.g., asking questions and defining problems) and home in on core ideas that will be necessary to understand the topic. In sum, phenomenon-driven activities are important enablers that anchor learning and establish why experiences that are both hands-on and minds-on are important.

Activity Box:
Planning for Engage Phase Activities

Driving questions for the Engage phase activities

- What science phenomena (or relevant life experience) can you use to hook students into the lesson?

- What specific ideas or misconceptions can you preassess during the Engage phase?

- What are the content-based learning targets for the lesson?

- What are the SEP and CC learning targets communicated to students?

- How can you motivate students and capture their attention?

- How do the engagement activities connect to students' lives?

Teacher Planning		Student Tasks	
"Emphasize now"	**"Highlight in another phase"**	**"Emphasize now"**	**"Highlight in another phase"**
• Motivate students and allow for a sense of wonder. • Focus learning. • Assess student understanding. • Cluster student ideas based on similarities and differences.	• Introduce science content, new terms, and concepts. • Grade student thinking.	• Share ideas. • Work individually or collaboratively. • Explain thinking.	• Look to outside sources for ideas.

Chapter 5

Consideration 4: Use Authoritative Explanations to Extend Learning
Students struggle with explaining complex scientific principles, and helping them co-construct these ideas during teacher explanations is a way to build their understanding. Thus, a key enabler to the 5E Model's success is the teacher's ability to provide explanations that support and build on students' evidence-based claims.

The teacher portion of the Explain phase is an excellent time to work together with students to create the rational portion of the C-E-R statement. From a cognitive standpoint, developing the reasoning with students in light of their evidence-based claims is a way to entrench ideas and help students develop sound reasoning skills and conceptual understanding. *America's Lab Report* (Singer, Hilton, and Schweingruber 2006) warned of the consequences of providing hands-on experiences that are disconnected from didactic instruction because doing so can create fragmented knowledge in students. Constructing the reasoning statement with students is a way to integrate labs with more didactic forms of instruction (e.g., lectures and textbook readings). Using teacher explanations to help students refine and elaborate their evidence-based claims is also a way to support their abilities in key SEPs (e.g., constructing explanations and communicating information) and is a building block for helping them engage in argumentation from evidence.

Activity Box:
Planning for Teacher Explain Phase

Driving questions for designing teacher Explain phase activities

- What underlying principles do you need to help students understand?

- What terms and concepts do you need to introduce that are essential for understanding?

- What other terms or ideas are directly related to the content and considered "nice to know," nonessential topics?

Teacher Planning		Student Tasks	
"Emphasize now"	"Highlight in another phase"	"Emphasize now"	"Highlight in another phase"
• Introduce terms, concepts, and ideas in light of student experiences.	• Explain content before students have a chance to articulate claims.	• Construct evidence-based claims.	• Try to generalize knowledge by testing ideas in other situations.
• Provide supporting content not easily observable firsthand.	• Provide all of the intended information on the subject.		
• Have students practice new ideas and terms.			
• Co-construct reasoning statements with students.			

Chapter 5

Consideration 5: Include Growth Indicators for Students and Teachers
The key to the Evaluate phase is not so much to develop a content knowledge test per se but to have kids show they can do science (i.e., they have gained abilities related to specific SEPs and CCs) and have learned disciplinary core ideas. Thus, from a backward design perspective, the evaluation is a key destination. The Evaluate phase is a chance for students to show that they know the intended content and have developed the ability to do science related to their experiences. In addition, this phase is a chance for students to reflect on their developing knowledge in important ways. Keep in mind that research has shown that using a metacognitive approach can have a great effect on student achievement and learning outcomes (Hattie 2009).

Evaluation activities might include having students think about whether they can apply problem-solving strategies in similar and different scenarios. Students might also consider whether they can question and target inadequacies in their own understanding and find experiences to remedy the situation. The ultimate goal of the student activities during the Evaluate phase is to help students reflect on whether the 5Es have helped them become more self-reliant learners.

Activity Box: Planning for Evaluate Phase Activities

Driving question for the Evaluate phase activities

- What summative assessment will teachers and students use to assess students' abilities and knowledge related to specific SEPs, CCs, and DCIs?

Teacher Planning		Student Tasks	
"Emphasize now"	**"Highlight in another phase"**	**"Emphasize now"**	**"Highlight in another phase"**
• Evaluate student understanding and learning. • Decide what content will be investigated next and how.	• Reteach content. • Provide differentiated learning environments so all students are proficient.	• Demonstrate understanding. • Reflect on how ideas have changed over time.	• Participate in remediation strategies to overcome inaccurate ideas.

Consideration 6: Provide Transferring Practice

Once your students have a solid explore–explain baseline of experiences for learning, you can create Elaborate phase activities that will allow them to develop knowledge at just the right time so they see the importance of using practices to learn science. Students can carry out elaboration activities that allow them to test their newly developed process and content ideas in a new and different scenario. Testing ideas in different contexts allows students to search for consistent outcomes. Students can also carry out elaborations that build on their knowledge of other related phenomena and with new and different targeted SEPs and CCs, to help them develop a deeper understanding of the science under study.

Activity Box:
Driving Questions for the Elaborate Phase

Driving questions for the Elaborate phase activities

- What hands-on investigation can students carry out to test an idea in a new situation or to build a new idea in a similar situation?

- What content-based learning targets are there for the Elaborate phase?

- What are the SEP and CC learning targets communicated to students?

Teacher Planning		Student Tasks	
"Emphasize now"	"Highlight in another phase"	"Emphasize now"	"Highlight in another phase"
• Provide specific learning activities to test ideas in new situations. • Offer procedural directives and safety information.	• Provide new lectures that elaborate on ideas thus far.	• Determine whether new ideas are generalizable given a different context. • Conduct library research on supporting ideas.	• Learn unrelated content.

Chapter 5

Conclusions

Regardless of the nature of the activities, the sequence of science instruction needs to be structured so that students are doing the intellectual work. Our job as *explore-before-explain* teachers is to develop or create experiences that allow students to make correct descriptions of the science phenomena under study. This planning step cannot be overemphasized. Identifying the phenomenon that students can make accurate evidence-based claims about is also critical because it underpins content learning and is the foundation for understanding how the practices of science can be used in a reliable way to understand the natural world. The link between content and process is vital because learning science processes takes place as students learn content. With a brief overview of *A Framework for K–12 Science Education* (National Research Council 2012) as a background, the model lessons that follow offer examples of how to put the vision of the reform into practice.

Chapter 6

Teaching About
Heat and Temperature
Using an Investigative
Demonstration

Chapter 6

I n professional development workshops and methods courses, I use this chapter as a starting point for eliciting elementary teachers' views of the effective sequencing of science instruction in classroom demonstrations. Many teachers already value minds-on experiences from demonstrations; however, they are unsure what knowledge students can construct. In addition, beginning elementary teachers are not sure when they need to provide explanations that build on students' experiences. After they try the lessons, I have found that many beginning elementary teachers have the same inaccurate conceptions that students have about thermal energy transfer.

This lesson is designed to anchor student learning around the following phenomenon: How does energy flow into, out of, or between an air-conditioned house and the outside during a hot summer day if the door to the house is left open? This is a confusing subject, and research has indicated that many students have trouble understanding that thermal energy naturally transfers from the warmer object to the colder object until both objects reach the same temperature (Keeley, Eberle, and Tugel 2007). I have created a lesson-level performance expectation (PE) to build students' understanding toward the broader expectation (i.e., the lesson-level PE is "make an evidence-based claim that energy can be moved from place to place by water"). By working together, teachers can create a dialogue with students about energy transfer. The model lesson highlights the connections of the learning activities to the three dimensions of *A Framework for K–12 Science Education* (National Research Council 2012), with specific footnotes that code the narrative to the science and engineering practices (SEPs) and crosscutting concepts (CCs).[1] This chapter is a tool for thinking strategically and helping teachers become more reflective practitioners.

---

1. The narrative portion in each of the model lessons is connected to the science and engineering practices and crosscutting concepts for grades 3–5 in Appendixes F and G, respectively, of the *NGSS* (NGSS Lead States 2013).

Activity Box: Using Formative Assessments to Drive Demonstrations

Use the activities below to reflect on the model lessons in Chapter 6. Go back and forth between your reflection journal and the model lessons. You can use the activities individually or as a group to reflect on how the POE (Predict, Observe, and Explain) sequence of instruction influences student learning.

1. Try out a model lesson from Chapter 6 (POE lesson) with a group of students or consider using the design structure and sequence for an activity of your own.

2. Reflect on students' responses to the lesson in terms of their motivation and learning. Think deeply about the research on cognition and sequence of instruction: How did the students react when you asked them to make predictions? List students' misconceptions and prior thoughts. Were their prior ideas similar to those identified in the model lesson? What were their observations and evidence-based claims?

3. Identify any salient research points you noticed when using the model lesson with students that you want to remember and use when designing your first POE lesson.

4. Brainstorm a list of upcoming demonstrations or student investigations you could sequence in a POE lesson.

5. Use the footnote connections to interpret how the narrative translates to the *Next Generation Science Standards* (*NGSS*).

Predict (3 to 4 minutes)

The demonstration begins by having students predict what will happen when two half-full beakers of water at different temperatures are mixed. Students' predictions are intimately connected to questions about what will happen when two different temperatures of water are mixed and tied back to the phenomenon driving the unit (i.e., transfer of thermal energy). I involve students in the investigation by having volunteers take the temperature of the two containers of water. Later on, students will continue to play an investigative role, collecting data to answer overarching questions about energy transfer.[2]

---

2. Students engage in SEPs and "ask questions that can be investigated and predict reasonable outcomes based on patterns such as cause and effect relationships" (NGSS Lead States 2013, p. 51).

Chapter 6

Students find that one beaker contains water at 30°C and the other beaker contains water at 15°C. At this point, students commit to their predictions by recording (on a whiteboard or a piece of paper) what they think the water temperature will be after the two beakers of water are combined (see Table 6.1). Predictions that are not graded encourage students to take a risk and communicate their scientific understanding of phenomena without having to worry about the grades they will receive for their ideas. Thus, our exploration is worthwhile because as a collective group we have varying ideas about what the temperature will be when different temperatures of water are mixed. We revisit our class graph often to reflect on whether our ideas change or stay the same based on the evidence we collect.

Table 6.1. *Students' Preconceptions and Postconceptions of Heat Transfer*

Conception	Preconceptions (*n* = 24) % (number of students)	Postconceptions (*n* = 24) % (number of students)
Subtraction	58% (14)	12% (3)
Average	21% (5)	88% (21)
Addition	8% (2)	0% (0)
Overriding	13% (3)	0% (0)

Note:
- The *subtraction* conception means that students thought that the lower-temperature water would be subtracted from the higher-temperature water.
- The *average* conception means that students thought that the two different temperatures of water would reach a temperature that is the average of the two different temperatures of water.
- The *addition* conception means that students thought that the two different temperatures of water would combine and equal a new temperature of water that is greater than the two containers of water individually.
- The *overriding* conception means that students thought that the higher temperature would prevail and be the resulting temperature.

Share (3 to 4 minutes)

During the next stage of the demonstration, students share their predictions with a partner and provide an explanation for their thinking while I circulate around the room and listen to their conversations. Through listening to students' explanations, I observe that some students believe their predictions to be accurate because their peers hold the same idea, while other students change their initial predictions based on their conversations, and some disagree with their partners and retain their initial conceptions.

At the end of the Share stage, students usually hold one of four conceptions of heat transfer. Most students think that the water temperature of the combined beakers will be 15°C. They explain that combining the two beakers will result in the colder water because "the 15°C water would be subtracted from the 30°C water." Some students think that the water temperature of the combined water will be 22°C. As one student explained, "The combined water temperature would be the temperature of the average between the two beakers." A few students think that combining the beakers will result in water that is 45°C, claiming that "the two water temperatures will add together." A few students think that the warmer water will override the cooler water and its temperature will prevail.

Observe (2 minutes)

During the Observe stage, students collect data to help them confirm, refute, or refine their scientific ideas. Next, I combine the two beakers of water and have a student volunteer take the temperature of the water, which is approximately 22°C.

It is important that during the Observe stage, students can make scientifically accurate claims based on evidence. Teachers should ensure when choosing two different temperatures of water that the difference between the two temperatures of water is not also the same as the average between the two temperatures of water. For example, if the demonstration involved water with temperatures of 5°C and 15°C, students would have difficulty formulating scientifically accurate conceptions from their observations because the difference (15°C – 5°C) and the average ([15°C + 5°C] / 2) both equal 10°C.

Explain (3 minutes)

During this stage, students provide an explanation for their observation that when equal amounts of 30°C and 15°C water combine, the resulting water temperature is approximately 22°C. It is important that students develop a written artifact so that they externalize their ideas in a concrete form. Individually, they write down on index cards their explanations and what they learned from the demonstration. I grade their responses on the spot during the Explain phase. Many students explain that the resulting water temperature is in the middle of the temperatures of the two combined containers of water.[3] We are building a context for sixth-grade mathematical explorations that ask students to be able to calculate the mean value in a data set (National Governors Association Center for Best Practices and Council of Chief State School Officers [NGAC and CCSSO] 2010).

Investigating Convection (5 to 7 minutes)

Because the mixing-water demonstration does not make this explicit, students have additional experiences to learn that the transfer of thermal energy naturally occurs only in one direction—from "warmer" to "colder" objects. The "Ice-Cold Lemonade"

---

3. Students' questions and data collection during the Predict and Observe phases, respectively, lead directly to an SEP in the Explain phase, and they "use evidence (e.g., measurements, observations, patterns) to construct or support an explanation" (NGSS Lead States 2013, p. 61).

Chapter 6

probe (*see next page*) addresses student prior knowledge and situates learning around a phenomenon related to thermal energy flow (Keeley, Eberle, and Tugel 2007). Students complete the probe as a worksheet that includes two parts: (1) a selected response and (2) critical thinking where students explain their reasoning. I ask students to read the probe individually.

After they individually read the probe, I read it out loud and explain what the probe is asking them to consider. I ask students to illustrate which choice they are selecting. Students use blue arrows to indicate if they think the coldness from the ice moved into the lemonade (Choice A). They use red arrows to indicate if they think the heat from the lemonade moved into the ice (Choice B). Students use blue arrows and red arrows, pointing in opposite directions, if they think the heat transferred both ways simultaneously (Choice C) (see Figure 6.1).

Figure 6.1. *Student Arrows to Show Predictions About Heat Transfer in the "Ice-Cold Lemonade" Probe*

Once students have made their choices, they each turn to a shoulder partner (two students total) and share their thinking. I give them some starter prompts to guide their conversations and join in with some probing questions:

T: *You've all seen ice in water. What do you think was happening?*

S: *I think it is because the heat … C makes me feel like it could be the answer. I don't think the coldness goes into the lemonade. I think something else makes it melt.*

T: *What else could make it melt?*

S: *I know the lemonade would make it melt because it is warmer than the ice. Also, if you left ice outside it would melt. So, I think the answer is either B or C.*

Ice-Cold Lemonade

It was a hot summer day. Mattie poured herself a glass of lemonade. The lemonade was warm, so Mattie put some ice in the glass. After 10 minutes, Mattie noticed that the ice was melting and the lemonade was cold. Mattie wondered what made the lemonade get cold. She had three different ideas. Which idea do you think best explains why the lemonade got cold? Circle your answer.

A The coldness from the ice moved into the lemonade.

B The heat from the lemonade moved into the ice.

C The coldness and the heat moved back and forth until the lemonade cooled off.

Explain your thinking. Describe the "rule" or reasoning you used for your answer.

_____

_____

_____

_____

_____

_____

_____

_____

_____

When I tally the student responses, most of the class thinks that the heat has transferred both ways. Nearly all of the students struggle to explain their thinking. They all know that holding a piece of ice made them feel cold, and over time the ice would melt; however, their lived experiences have not provided the evidence on the direction that heat transfers. Thus, the goal is to give them a lived experience in which to form accurate science understanding.

SAFETY NOTES

1. Wear sanitized, indirectly vented chemical splash safety goggles, a nonlatex apron, and thick heat-resistant gloves during the setup, hands-on, and take-down segments of the activity, for both students and teacher.
2. Immediately wipe up any liquid spilled on the floor—a slip-and-fall hazard.
3. Use caution when working with glassware. It can potentially cut or puncture skin.
4. Have direct adult supervision if you are working with glassware and hot liquids.
5. Wash hands with soap and water after completing this activity.

Data-Producing Experience (10 minutes)

At this point, students are inquisitive about which direction heat transfers. The assessment probe easily lends itself to similar situations that are testable and could produce the data the class needs. I tell the class that we are going to create a scientific model to help us explain and test our predictions about the direction that heat transfers. Using an Erlenmeyer flask, a beaker, hot water, cold water, red food coloring, and blue food coloring, we set out to answer which way heat transfers. We have two setups: (1) place hot water in the Erlenmeyer flask and dye it red, and place it in a beaker of cold water that was not dyed; and (2) place cold water in the Erlenmeyer flask and dye it blue, and place it in a beaker of hot water that was not dyed. (As a note to teachers, the "hot water" was 65.5°C and the cold water was 9.5°C.) Once students understand the experimental setup, we compare the different components with the assessment probe to identify how our investigation will allow us to know which way heat transfers.

The demonstration allows students to visualize heat transfer and have a model of phenomena not readily observable firsthand. As a model, the demonstration allows for predictive value as well as an explanation of science. To students' surprise, heat transfers in only one direction, from hot to cold (see Figures 6.2 and 6.3).

Students have no evidence from the model that heat transferred from cold to hot or in both directions at the same time. We videotape the models so we can revisit them and observe them more closely. (For teachers who do not have the supplies, you can use the video found here: *www.youtube.com/watch?v=xLA1EiXUCuM.*)

Students' Evidence-Based Claims (25 minutes)

The model provides the qualitative evidence that students need to develop knowledge of the assessment probe. Once students have the evidence, they write claims based on evidence statements to articulate their thinking. For example, students have written that "heat transfers from hot to cold but not cold to hot" and that the model "showed that only the warm water dyed red moved into the cold water. Cold water dyed blue did not move into the surrounding warm water."

Authoritative Explanation

Students' evidence-based claims serve as the conceptual framework for introducing new ideas. As a whole group, we talk about why heat transfers in one direction. One student described the transfer of energy phenomenon using the analogy of running a race. She explained, "Like people in a race, when a slower person is running with a faster person, the slower one is going to want to catch up. So, the slower one speeds up so they are going the same speed as the faster one." I asked, "But where would the energy come from so the slower one can speed up?" I told students to think about the runner in terms of the demonstration and what we found out. Another student chimed in and remarked that, in this example, "the slower runner can't just catch up, it gets energy from the faster runner. The faster runner gets slower and the slower runner gets faster to even the race out." The students liked this analogy and agreed that the faster goes a little slower and the slower goes a little faster.

We looked at the demonstrations from a microscopic perspective and noted that the water of different temperatures is made of molecules too small to be seen. We turned the running analogy into a scientific reasoning statement and exchanged the idea of

Figure 6.2. *Student Observations of Heat Transfers*

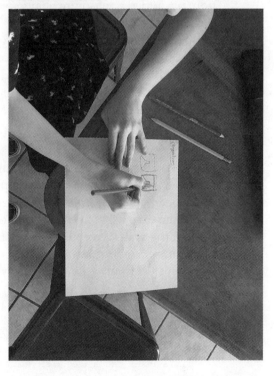

Figure 6.3. *A Student Drawing Observations Based on Evidence*

the runners with the temperature of molecules. Students wrote that the hot molecules with more energy transfer energy to the cold molecules with less energy. Over time, all of the molecules would have the same energy. The warm molecules have more energy than the colder molecules. When molecules collide, they transfer energy from hot to cold (PS3.B Energy Transfer; NGSS Lead States 2013).

We acted out the molecular movement in our classroom using what we term *pretend modeling*.[4] Half of the students represented hot molecules and the other half represented cold molecules. I had students each face a partner and act out the relative molecular movements. In the class, the students who represented hot molecules moved faster than the cold molecules. Next, I had the same pairs of partners all raise both hands. We pretended that our fingertips were molecules. One partner's fingertips were hot molecules and the other partner's fingertips were cold molecules. Again, we used pretend modeling to show how energy is transferred from hot to cold until all molecules have the same temperature. Students modeled this by the gradual slowing down of hot molecules and the gradual speeding up of cold molecules.[5]

The molecular discussion was just one step toward helping students develop knowledge, and this would be a reoccurring topic with our course. With this explanation, we added a reasoning statement describing the models on the molecular level to the students' evidence-based claim. The explanation helped tie together the overarching principles associated with energy transfer on the microscopic level. Adding concrete details to their claims-evidence-reasoning statement had a nice carryover effect to English language arts and helped students write a complete explanation of the science under study (CCSS.ELA-Literacy.W.5.2.B; CCSS.ELA-Literacy.W.5.2.E; NGAC and CCSSO 2010).

Follow-Up Assessments

More than 10 weeks after I first taught the thermal energy lesson (24 weeks into the semester), students completed the paper-and-pencil formative assessment worksheet described by Keeley, Eberle, and Tugel (2007) as part of an end-of-semester assessment. The formative assessment worksheet asked students to predict what the temperature of the water would be when two half-full glasses of water of the same size—one containing 50°C water and the other containing 10°C water—are combined and to provide reasoning for their answer. Students had the following selected-response

---

4. Students wiggle their fingers to simulate molecular motion. They are using the SEP of modeling and "develop and/or use models to describe and/or predict phenomena" (NGSS Lead States 2013, p. 53). Modeling is a theme of how they can explain science and is direct evidence for the CC they use throughout the class. Students' models "can be used to represent systems and their interactions—such as students learn matter is made of particles and energy can be transferred in various ways and between objects" (NGSS Lead States 2013, p. 86). Finally, the modeling activities directly tie to another SEP, and students "communicate scientific and/or technical information orally and/or in written formats" (NGSS Lead States 2013, p. 65).

5. Students' experiences with thermal energy relate to many themes in physical science, and their experiences provide additional evidence for the CC that states, "Students learn matter is made of particles and energy can be transferred in various ways and between objects" (NGSS Lead States 2013, p. 85).

answers: (a) 20°C, (b) 30°C, (c) 40°C, (d) 50°C, and (e) 60°C. (See Keeley, Eberle, and Tugel 2007 for the full formative assessment probe worksheet.)

I also added a second selected-response item to the formative assessment probe worksheet, in which students identified the direction in which heat is naturally transferred: (a) only from "hot" to "cold," (b) only from "cold" to "hot," (c) both directions simultaneously, and (d) none of the above. When I assessed students' responses, I was pleased by their ideas, given that many students' initial misconceptions about energy transfer are persistent and survive in spite of learning about these concepts (Driver et al. 1994).

Most students selected 30°C and reasoned that "when two temperatures are mixed together, they even out" and that they "found the middle between the two different temperatures." Some students still thought that "you take the higher temperature (50°C) and minus the lower temperature (10°C) and they equal 40°C." Very few students thought that the temperature would be 60°C. In addition, most students held scientifically accurate postconceptions of heat transferring naturally only from "hot" to "cold" (see Table 6.2).

Table 6.2. *Students' Postconceptions of the Direction in Which Heat Transfers*

Postconceptions	Breakdown of Student Responses (*n* = 24) % (number of students)
"Hot" to "cold"	83% (20)
"Cold" to "hot"	4% (1)
Both directions	13% (3)
None of the above	0% (0)

Although teachers would expect that students would learn this content after being taught it, the small number of students with inaccurate conceptions speaks to the resiliency of students' misconceptions in spite of firsthand experiences learning content. For most students, the experiences in the PSOE (Predict-Share-Observe-Explain) lesson helped them develop long-lasting, scientifically accurate conceptions of heat transfer. This lesson also addresses the three dimensions of the *NGSS* (see the *NGSS* connections in Table 6.3, p. 64).

Chapter 6

Table 6.3. *Unwrapping the* Explore-Before-Explain *Energy Transfer Investigation in Chapter 6*

Energy	Connections to Classroom Activity
Performance Expectation	
4-PS3-2: Make observations to provide evidence that energy can be transferred from place to place by sound, light, heat, and electric currents.	Students investigate the transfer of thermal energy using food coloring and different temperatures of water (hot vs. cold).
Science and Engineering Practices	
Asking questions and defining problems	Students make predictions about how different water temperatures interact when they encounter each other.
Analyzing and interpreting data	Students use qualitative data from their observations of the demonstration to learn which direction thermal energy transfers.
Developing and using models	Students use water that is colored using dye as a model for understanding how heat transfers.
Constructing explanations and designing solutions	Students formulate claims based on evidence statements.
Disciplinary Core Ideas	
PS3.A: Definitions of Energy: Energy can be moved from place to place by moving objects or through sound, light, or electric currents.	Students observe that when different temperatures of water that has been dyed with food coloring come into contact with each other, water moves from areas that are "hot" to "cold."
PS3.B: Energy Transfer: Energy is present whenever there are moving objects, sound, light, or heat. When objects collide, energy can be transferred from one object to another, thereby changing their motion. In such collisions, some energy is typically also transferred to the surrounding air; as a result, the air gets heated and sound is produced.	Students talk about motion energy on a molecular level and compare the movement of molecules for "hot" versus "cold" water.
Crosscutting Concepts	
Systems and system modeling	Students investigate how "warm" water and "cold" water interact. They use food coloring as a tool for learning how energy is transferred between "warm" and "cold" water.
Energy and matter: Flow, cycles, and conservation	Students track the flow of movement of thermal energy to understand how heat transfers in a system.

Note: The materials, lessons, and activities outlined in this chapter are just one step toward reaching the performance expectation listed in this table. Additional supporting materials, lessons, and activities will be required. See *www.nextgenscience.org/msps-e-energy* for more information.

Chapter 7

Investigating Change Using the Invisible Test Tube Demonstration

Activity Box:
Exploring the POE Model Lessons

Use the activities below to reflect on the model lessons in Chapter 7. Go back and forth between your reflection journal and the model lessons. You can use the activities individually or as a group to reflect on how the POE (Predict, Observe, and Explain) sequence of instruction influences student learning.

1. Try out a model lesson from Chapter 7 (POE lesson) with a group of students.

2. Reflect on students' reactions to any surprising occurrences or discrepant events that happen during the demonstration. How might starting lessons with discrepant events influence student motivation and learning?

3. Think deeply about how students can use crosscutting concepts to explore phenomena: "What patterns do I notice in this phenomenon?" "What are the components of the phenomenon, and how do they interact?" "What happens when I change some conditions of the phenomenon while others stay stable?"

4. How could you extend and add activities so that the model lessons conform to a 5E (Engage, Explore, Explain, Elaborate, Evaluate) instructional sequence?

5. Brainstorm a list of upcoming phenomena you could use to sequence in a POE lesson.

6. Use the footnote connections to interpret how the narrative translates to the *Next Generation Science Standards* (*NGSS*).

An important theme throughout the chapters so far has been the complex interplay among learning, cognition, and instructional sequences. You can use your knowledge of learners and learning and the research as your reason to become an *explore-before-explain* teacher.

Before jumping into the model lesson in this chapter, I want to suggest some precautions. Keep in mind that "off-the-shelf" lessons do not help teachers apply strategies proven to increase student learning. Revisit Chapters 1–3 to reflect on the phases and activities to think about and spark conversations with your peers regarding how to sequence science instruction in meaningful ways. Just as we want our students to make evidence-based claims in our classes, use your personal experiences and ideas about learners and learning from the research to support your professional development.

The model lesson in this chapter is aimed at explaining why objects appear different underwater versus out in the open. If you have experienced this phenomenon, it is because light rays are influenced by different substances (such as air and water) depending on the substance's physical properties. The word *refraction* describes the phenomenon of light rays bending as they pass from one substance to another substance. Although many students experience the property of refraction in everyday life, research has indicated that they have difficulty explaining how light rays are influenced by different mediums (Driver et al. 1994).

What follows is a PSOE (Predict-Share-Observe-Explain) demonstration that I use to captivate students in learning the performance expectation that states they "develop a model to describe that light reflecting from objects and entering the eye allows objects to be seen" (4-PS4-2; NGSS Lead States 2013). In addition, these activities highlight *A Framework for K–12 Science Education* (National Research Council 2012) and the *NGSS* (NGSS Lead States 2013) (see the connections in the footnotes for explicit relationships between the activities and the science and engineering practices and crosscutting concepts). In these activities, students engage in essential practices while they work collaboratively to formulate ideas and analyze, interpret, and make scientific claims based on data.

Predict

The lesson begins by having students make a prediction about how different substances change the behavior of light. Teachers can help elicit students' ideas about the behavior of light by asking them to think about how different mediums influence how objects appear. I use three different setups that will be revealed during the Observe stage of the demonstration: (1) an empty test tube placed in an empty 50 ml beaker, (2) a test tube filled nearly to the top with water submerged in a 50 ml beaker filled with water, and (3) a test tube filled nearly to the top with cooking oil in a 50 ml beaker of cooking oil (Wesson-brand cooking oil works well for the demonstration).

At this point in the demonstration, it is beneficial to have an empty test tube and beaker, a beaker with water, a test tube with water, a beaker with oil, and a test tube with oil available to support visual learners. The test tubes are not in the beakers at this point. Next, students individually record their predictions on sticky notes as a way to commit to an idea and make their conceptions explicit. Having students write down their ideas makes their thinking concrete, and they can revisit their initial conceptions later in the lesson. Students' written predictions are not graded during this stage, so they will feel comfortable expressing their conceptions of science phenomena.

Chapter 7

Share

The next phase of the lesson provides students with collaborative opportunities to share their thinking. During this time, they each tell a partner sitting close by what they predict they will see when two different setups are unveiled. In addition, students give reasons for their predictions and explain their thinking. They mark on their PSOE worksheets whether their ideas are similar to or different from their peers' ideas. Students do not need long to share their ideas, and a short amount of time ensures that their conversations stay on task; two minutes total (one minute for each partner) is sufficient. Once the students have shared their ideas with their partners, the teacher can quickly go around the room and have students say "same" or "different" (to indicate whether the students' ideas were the same as or different from their partners' ideas). This is a quick check to make sure that all students shared ideas.

Next, the teacher can have a whole-group discussion (5–10 minutes) to allow students to share ideas. Students are encouraged to engage in discussion and provide explanations from their everyday experiences for their ideas. The teacher should remain an active listener during this discussion, encouraging students to talk with each other but not providing feedback indicating whether the students' conceptions are correct. The teacher should be aware that students could develop inaccurate ideas based on discussions with their classmates, and some will assert that they know what will happen from prior experiences; however, I find that the latter is rarely the case. Therefore, at this point in the PSOE sequence, I do not grade students' predictions.

At the end of the Share stage, I have students draw and label in their notebooks what they think is happening in the different situations that explains their predictions. Student illustrations should include their predictions and explanations. I ask students in their explanations to represent how light waves and different materials might interact to explain their predictions. I also explicitly make connections between student models in this activity and how we use models in science to explain and make predictions about how the world works. Thus, students see that their modeling activity not only helps them understand the science under study but also helps them think logically about science.[1] Each of the scenarios helps anchor learning around how different materials influence how an object looks. Most students believe that when the empty test tube is placed in an empty beaker, the test tube will appear to be the exact same size (in other words, they think there will be no change). See Figure 7.1.

Figure 7.1. *Student Prediction About Empty Test Tube in Empty Beaker*

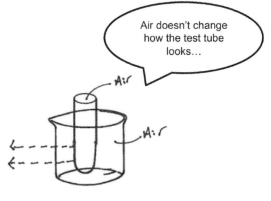

---

1. Students use a science and engineering practice (SEP) and a crosscutting concept (CC) that support one another. They "develop and/or use models to describe and/or predict phenomena" (NGSS Lead States 2013, p. 53), which supports the CC that students can "describe a system in terms of its components and their interactions" (NGSS Lead States 2013, p. 85).

Figure 7.2. *Student Prediction About Test Tube With Water in Beaker With Water*

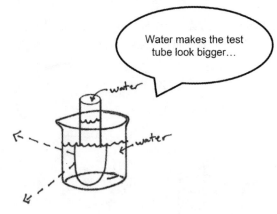

Teachers will also find that most students think that the portion of the test tube filled with water submerged in a beaker with water will look magnified. For example, some students will draw a test tube filled with water in a beaker filled with water larger than the actual test tube and use lines to represent rays of light (see Figure 7.2).

Students explain that the water acts as a magnifying glass and causes light rays to spread out, making the test tube appear larger than it actually is. They support their ideas with their real-life experiences. One of my students talked about how a spoon placed in a glass of water appears to be magnified. Others have mentioned that when looking at a coin in water from above, the coin appears to be larger than it actually is.

Students are less sure about what will happen when a test tube filled with oil is placed in a beaker of oil. They draw on their knowledge of the properties of liquids to formulate predictions about the oil and glass. Most students draw on their experiences looking at objects underwater and predict that the submerged portion of the test tube will appear to be either larger or smaller than the actual test tube. These students' drawings reveal their beliefs that (1) oil will cause light rays to spread out, making the test tube look bigger; or (2) oil will cause light rays to bend inward, causing the object to appear to be smaller (see Figures 7.3 and 7.4).

Some students think that the submerged portion of the test tube will be difficult to see and claim that the outline of the test tube will be "blurry" and unclear (see Figure 7.5, p. 70).

Figure 7.3. *Student Prediction About Test Tube With Oil in Beaker With Oil*

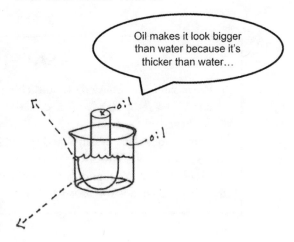

Figure 7.4. *Student Prediction About Test Tube With Oil in Beaker With Oil*

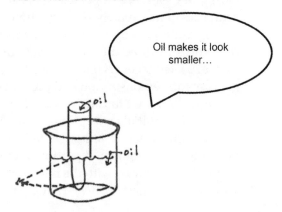

Chapter 7

Figure 7.5. *Another Student Prediction About Test Tube With Oil in Beaker With Oil*

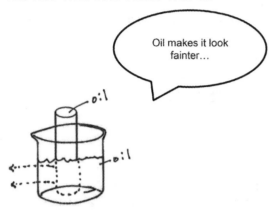

These students explain that the density of the oil will block some light from traveling through the beaker, making it difficult to see the test tube. Students' drawings show light rays becoming fainter as they enter the oil (some of my students have illustrated this by showing a thick line turning into a dotted line when the light ray enters the oil). If students have similar conceptions, the teacher may find it helpful to tally their ideas on the front board for everyone to see. The result of the Share stage is that students change, revise, elaborate, or retain their initial conceptions based on their conversations with their peers.

SAFETY NOTES

1. Wear sanitized, indirectly vented chemical splash safety goggles and a nonlatex apron during the setup, hands-on, and take-down segments of the activity, for both students and teacher.
2. Immediately wipe up any liquid spilled on the floor—a slip-and-fall hazard.
3. Use caution when working with glassware. It can potentially cut or puncture skin.
4. Have direct adult supervision if you are working with glassware and hot liquids.
5. Wash your hands with soap and water after completing this activity.

Observe

During the Observe stage, teachers can get students excited by unveiling each of the setups at approximately the same time. One way to ensure student engagement is by having multiple setups for the students to observe. For example, the teacher can bring the setups to three different stations in the room. It is important that the students remain seated so everyone can see the demonstration. This will allow all students to observe the demonstration and prevent disruptions.

Students are not too surprised when an empty test tube is placed in an empty beaker and their initial conceptions are verified that the test tube will look the same (see the YouTube video at *https://youtu.be/MjlTP_2sy7s*). Many students are surprised by how much the submerged portion of the water-filled test tube in the beaker of water is magnified compared with the nonsubmerged section of the test tube (see the YouTube video at *https://youtu.be/3N6_UkJQZ6o*). See Figure 7.6.

Students write on their PSOE worksheet what they observe and record whether their prediction was supported or disconfirmed. They are then able to revise the models they had drawn in their notebooks during the Share phase. I mention to students that for us to be able to see an object, light rays have to bounce off the object and return to the eye (i.e., reflection). I challenge students to show in their drawings how light rays bounce off the test tube and travel back to their eyes. At this point in the Observe stage, students are pleased to find that their predictions are accurate.

When the third setup is revealed, the energy, enthusiasm, and interest in the room quickly reach a new height (see the YouTube video at *https://youtu.be/jFXXvhc3zSc*). Students' eyes widen and their jaws drop, and they are completely shocked by the results. It is rare for a single student to have an accurate prediction. See Figure 7.7.

Students notice that in this setup, the submerged portion of the test tube appears to be invisible. To achieve maximum engagement from students without disruption, the teacher should unveil the demonstrations as close to the same time as possible. Some students react to the demonstration by saying that it's a magic trick. They claim that the "test tube is broken" and that they are being "tricked" by the teacher. Some students believe the test tube does not actually have a submerged portion and is possibly a broken test tube resting on top of the oil. However, when the test tube is lifted out of the oil by the teacher and the students see that it is a whole, unbroken test tube, they are stunned. When the test tube filled with oil is placed back in the beaker with oil, the submerged portion of the test tube again disappears. This part of the demonstration gets a lot of "wows," "oohs," and "ahs."

At the end of the Observe stage, students write down what they observed for each of the demonstrations, record whether their initial predictions were supported based on the demonstration, and explain what changed in the two setups. By introducing the idea that seeing an object is related to light rays bouncing off the object (i.e., reflection), the demonstration helps students revise their drawings for the test tube in a beaker of oil. With guidance, the students draw light rays passing through the test tube in a beaker of oil with no light rays being reflected (see Figure 7.8, p. 72).

Figure 7.6. *Water-Filled Test Tube Submerged in a Beaker of Water*

Figure 7.7. *Oil-Filled Test Tube Submerged in a Beaker of Oil*

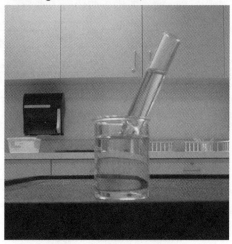

Chapter 7

Figure 7.8. *Student Drawing That Explains Test Tube With Oil in Beaker With Oil*

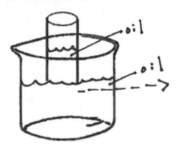

This is an excellent opportunity to illustrate to students how small changes in the system can dramatically influence their perception of objects, because it is not until the test tubes are submerged in the beakers that the test tubes look different. Teachers can challenge students to think about how science can be thought of as a system. The class discusses how systems are composed of many factors and variables that are smaller subcomponents. Understanding the subcomponents and their interrelationships is important for gaining a deeper conceptual understanding of science.

Explain

In this lesson, students use a table that has been modified from their textbook (Padilla, Miaoulis, and Cyr 2007) and that includes the refractive index of Pyrex glass (i.e., the beaker and test tube). (The data needed to create such a table are available in the textbook and at *www.pgo-online.com/intl/katalog/pyrex.html*; see Table 7.1.)

Table 7.1. *Refractive Indexes*

Material	Approximate Refractive Index
Air (gas)	1.00
Water (liquid)	1.33
Corn oil (liquid)	1.47
Pyrex glass (solid)	1.47

Students find patterns in the data that help them make sense of the two setups in the demonstration. First, students infer from the data that the value of the refractive index is an indicator of how much a material bends light. Substances with refractive indexes that are close to 1, such as air, do not noticeably bend light. Hence, when the test tube is placed in an empty beaker, it appears to be the exact same size. Second, students are able to make scientific claims about how refractive indexes that deviate from a value of 1 influence the bending of light. Students use the refractive index of water (1.33) and Pyrex glass (1.47) to make the scientific claim that as the value of the refractive index deviates from a value of 1, the amount that light bends changes. Thus, water (1.33) and Pyrex glass (1.47) bend light more than air (1.00). This is evidenced by students' firsthand experiences in which the submerged portion of the test tube in water appeared to be magnified.

The most difficult concept for students to understand is the third setup: the test tube filled with oil submerged in a beaker of oil. Students benefit from working in pairs to explain how the refractive indexes of cooking oil and Pyrex glass relate to what they observed about the combination of these materials in the demonstration. Students observe from data that the indexes of refraction for cooking oil and Pyrex glass are virtually the same (both are approximately 1.47). From their firsthand experiences with the demonstration and from data, the students are able to infer that when the refractive indexes of two materials are the same, an object can seem invisible. Thus, the students explain that the matching refractive indexes is the factor that changed in the demonstration and is the reason that the submerged portion of the test tube appears to be invisible.

Once students have had an opportunity to formulate an explanation, the teacher can support their understanding. Students learn that the matching refractive indexes remove reflections (when some light bounces back) and refractions (when light bends) where the test tube and oil meet. As a result of removing the reflection and refraction of light, there is no visible boundary between the test tube and the oil. The object seems invisible because light transmits through it without bending, bouncing back, or being absorbed (these ideas are connected to the student drawings; see Figure 7.8). To support this idea, teachers can place another object with a different refractive index than water, oil, or Pyrex glass, such as a metal spoon, in the oil. The teacher may find it helpful for students to draw their predictions, including light rays and reflected light, in their notes. After students have drawn their predictions, they should discuss their ideas and provide evidence for their thinking.[2]

Students will observe that the spoon in the oil is visible because it reflects and absorbs light. The teacher can also place a test tube of water in the beaker of oil so the students can see mismatched indexes of refraction. They will observe that the test tube of water looks magnified when placed in the beaker of oil. Finally, the teacher can further extend student learning by discussing real-life examples that use this principle. For example, camera lenses use matching refractive indexes to reduce the reflection of light to lessen the glare on an object and to allow photographers to capture fine details and colors of objects.

The end result of this lesson is that students gain a deeper understanding of how different materials influence how objects appear. This lesson also addresses all three dimensions of the *NGSS* (see *NGSS* connections in Table 7.2, p. 74).

---

2. The students use three interrelated SEPs to gain deeper conceptual understanding. First, they "analyze and interpret data to make sense of phenomena, using logical reasoning" (NGSS Lead States 2013, p. 57). Next, they "use evidence (e.g., measurements, observations, patterns) to construct or support an explanation or design a solution to a problem" (NGSS Lead States 2013, p. 61). Finally, they "communicate scientific and/or technical information orally and/or in written formats" (NGSS Lead States 2013, p. 65).

Table 7.2. *Unwrapping the Standards in Chapter 7*

Waves and Their Applications in Technologies for Information Transfer	Connections to Classroom Activity
Performance Expectation	
4-PS4-2: Develop a model to describe that light reflecting from objects and entering the eye allows objects to be seen.	During the demonstration, students create and revise models showing how light behaves when it encounters different mediums.
Science and Engineering Practices	
Analyzing and interpreting data	First, students make qualitative observations about the two different demonstrations. Second, they use data tables to better understand how different mediums influence light.
Developing and using models	Students create a picture with labels as a way to model their thinking about how different mediums influence the behavior of light. After students observe the demonstrations firsthand, they revise their initial models of the demonstration. Students test the reliability of their models in additional demonstrations involving mediums with mismatched refractive indexes.
Constructing explanations and designing solutions	Students make evidence-based claims for how objects can be made to seem invisible. First, they think about the factors that are similar and different between the two demonstrations. Second, they use quantitative data about the refractive indexes of different materials to explain how different mediums bend light. Students connect quantitative and qualitative data to explain how a refractive index of close to 1 does not noticeably bend light and how materials with matching refractive indexes can be coordinated to make an object look invisible.
Obtaining, evaluating, and communicating information	Students use prior experiences to explain to each other what will happen when objects with different refractive indexes (metal spoon and oil) are placed together.
Disciplinary Core Idea	
PS4.B: Electromagnetic Radiation: An object can be seen when light reflected from its surface enters the eyes.	Students' models of the behavior of light illustrate that light travels in a straight line through air but bends when it encounters a new and different medium (e.g., glass, water, oil).

Continued

Table 7.2. (*continued*)

Waves and Their Applications in Technologies for Information Transfer	Connections to Classroom Activity
Crosscutting Concepts	
Patterns	Students look for patterns in the refractive indexes table to understand how much different mediums bend (or refract) light.
Systems and systems models	Initially, students create pictures with labels that explain their predictions and observations.

Note: The materials, lessons, and activities outlined in this chapter are just one step toward reaching the performance expectation listed in this table. Additional supporting materials, lessons, and activities will be required. See *www.nextgenscience.org/msps-e-energy* for more information.

Chapter 8

There's More to Magnetism Than Objects Being Attracted to Refrigerators

Chapter 8

Many teachers find it difficult to connect assessments to evaluate students' prior knowledge with exploratory activities. Even experienced teachers are sometimes unsure of what to do with students' ideas and want to jump right in and address misconceptions by telling students the accurate ideas. This chapter explores a phenomenon related to the lesson title—"Why do certain objects stick to the refrigerator?"—and begins with an engagement activity that uses formative assessments to evaluate students' ideas about magnets. The chapter provides the foundation for exploring why starting with students' ideas and explorations is important in science learning, and it shows teachers how they can straightforwardly connect scientific explanations to students' misconceptions and experiences.

Specific assessment probes and typical student responses help teachers make sense of typical student ideas during all phases of instruction. This chapter highlights how teachers can continue to build students' conceptual knowledge in new and different situations to help students develop deeper understanding. After trying the lessons with students, teachers can reflect on how this approach is similar to and different from how they have traditionally approached the topic in the past. The chapter includes many connections, shown in the footnotes, to the three dimensions of the *NGSS*.

Engage

When the 5E lesson commenced, students were beginning a unit on magnetism. My goals for the Engage phase were fourfold: (1) assess students' prior knowledge and misconceptions of magnetism topics, (2) initiate the learning task, (3) focus student learning on measurable outcomes, and (4) engage and motivate students in the lesson and unit.

The Engage phase occurred during a session of "bell work" (transition time at the beginning of class) during which students completed two different formative assessment probes. The first assessment probe asked students to decide which of four different student explanations accurately describes the magnetic forces between magnets and paper clips in air or in water (see Table 8.1 and Keeley and Tugel 2009, p. 67).

Table 8.1. *Formative Assessment Probe, "Magnets in Water," and Student Ideas*

Selected Response Items[a]	Student Responses (*n* = 36)	Representative Written Explanations of Student Thinking
"I think magnets and paper clips need to be in air. If both the magnets and the paper clips are in water, they won't attract."	11% (4)	"They don't attract if something is between them."
"I think magnets need to be in the air, but it doesn't matter if the paper clip is. Magnets can attract paper clips covered in water."	6% (2)	"I think if a magnet is in water, it will not work."
"I don't think air makes a difference. I think magnets will attract paper clips when both are underwater."	58% (21)	"Magnets don't work any different in water. It's just like having it out of water. It will attract."
"I don't think air makes a difference. However, when magnets are in water, they work the opposite way. The paper clips will be repelled by the magnet."	25% (9)	"I think that if both the magnet and paper clips are underwater, they will repel instead of attract." "I think the water will make the magnet push away the paper clip."

[a] From Keeley and Tugel 2009, p. 67.

I was not overly surprised by my students' preconceptions about magnets and their properties given the National Science Education Standards content standards for elementary student learning and typical student misconceptions (National Research

Council [NRC] 1996; see Table 8.2). Approximately half of my students (53%) held accurate conceptions of how magnetic forces travel through both air and water.

Table 8.2. *Elementary and Middle School Students' Conceptions of Magnetism*

• The *National Science Education Standards* suggest that students begin exploring magnetism in K–4 science activities and learn that "magnets attract and repel each other and certain kinds of other materials" (NRC 1996, p. 127).
• Many elementary students observe that materials that are magnetic have forces that can interact without the materials touching each other (Keeley and Tugel 2009).

Table 8.1 (p. 79) shows students' selected responses to the first assessment probe and representative written explanations of their thinking about magnetic forces.

The second assessment probe asked students to generate a list of objects in the science classroom they thought were magnetic or not magnetic and state the rule that they used to make their decision (Table 8.3). While students eagerly went about their task, I circulated the room and checked to make sure that all students had answered these initial questions.

Table 8.3. *Results of Formative Assessment Probe to Determine Students' Conceptions of Magnetic Materials*

Magnetic Items	Nonmagnetic Items	Representative "Rules" Students Used to Determine Whether an Object Was Magnetic
File cabinet drawer Staples Door handle Cabinet handles Spoon Paper clip Nail Pushpin	Cabinet Lab table Door Whiteboard Binder Pencil Felt Book Poster Wooden shelf Plastic chair Cup Floor Plastic trash can Tissue	"If the object can attract certain types of metal, it's magnetic." "If it looks metal, then it is magnetic, but if it looks like plastic or paper, then it is not magnetic." "If it has metal in it or is made of something magnetic, then it is magnetic." "To be magnetic it must be copper, nickel, or zinc."

There's More to Magnetism Than Objects Being Attracted to Refrigerators

In the second assessment probe, most students reasoned that metal objects are magnetic. They listed metal items in the classroom as being magnetic and nonmetal items as being nonmagnetic based on this reasoning. Table 8.3 shows the cumulative list of materials that students identified as being magnetic or nonmagnetic and representative "rules" that they used to determine whether an object was magnetic or not.

During a whole-class discussion after they had completed the assessment, students made connections between certain materials and the list they had constructed. For instance, they noted that door and cabinet handles appeared to be made from the same types of metal. The students were also able to identify that not all metal objects in the room contained the same type of metal and that a penny contained a different metal than either the door or cabinet handles.

SAFETY NOTES

1. Wear sanitized, indirectly vented chemical splash safety goggles or safety glasses with side shields and a nonlatex apron during the setup, hands-on, and take-down segments of the activity, for both students and teacher.
2. Immediately wipe up any liquid spilled on the floor—a slip-and-fall hazard.
3. Have direct adult supervision if you are working with magnets.
4. Use caution when working with sharp items such as pins and needles. They can puncture or scrape skin.
5. Wash your hands with soap and water after completing this activity.

Explore

My goals for the Explore phase were to provide students with opportunities to test ideas with their peers, to develop a common base of understanding about the materials we were investigating, and to give individual students a chance to think and make predictions about these materials. I wanted to build on students' prior knowledge so they could develop deeper understandings about why certain materials are magnetic and how the forces interact between magnetic materials.

I began by asking the students to make a prediction about whether all of the materials they identified as magnetic or not magnetic would be attracted to a bar magnet. Once everyone had made predictions about the materials, I tallied the students' results on the board. Everyone thought all the metal objects would be magnetic. In addition, most students thought the nonmetals would not be attracted to the magnet. The class list represents a common theme in the course, and we frequently use patterns in data as the basis for our scientific claims.

Once all of the students had made predictions about all of the objects, I provided teams of students with bar magnets. I asked students to test their ideas and to revise

Chapter 8

the rule they used to explain whether materials are magnetic based on the data they collected. I mentioned that although the safety concerns were minimal, they needed to handle sharp objects (a pushpin and a nail) carefully. While the students tested their predictions, I circulated the room, going to each team of students and asking probing questions to extend the experience.[1] For example, I asked students whether magnetism can pass through paper, a notebook, and the wooden tabletop and whether a paper clip and a magnet would be attracted to each other if they were both under water. Students eagerly tested these ideas.

Explain

Once all students had collected data to test their predictions, I returned to the data table on the front board and added a column to their predicted results titled "Actual Results." As a class, we tallied the actual results. The students thought it was interesting that most metal objects, except for a metal spoon and a door handle, were attracted to the magnet and that none of the nonmetals were attracted to the magnet. Students began to revise their initial thoughts about magnets generated from our class list. In this way, they learned that the accumulation of data could help revise and elaborate our evidence-based claims.

I deemed that it was time to discuss the big ideas as a whole group and invited students to explain what they knew about the properties of magnets. The students observed from the data they collected that not all metals are magnetic, or as one student put it, "the metal in the spoon must be a type of metal that is not magnetic." I was pleased with this statement because it was a scientific claim that the student had made from evidence collected. Some students now remembered that only certain types of metals are magnetic. A student noted, "I think metals have to have iron in them to be magnetic. The spoon and door handle must not have iron in them." Another student asked if we could test metals that did not contain iron. Using a soda can and a penny, students tested the "iron hypothesis" and found that both the soda can and the penny were not attracted to the magnet.

During the whole-group discussion, I also asked whether magnetism could travel through different objects. One team noticed that magnetism could travel through paper (the textbook) and water but not through the wooden tabletop. A student suggested, "We need a more powerful magnet for it to travel through the thick tabletop." Thus, students' discussions required them to make a claim based on evidence and to develop scientific explanations for phenomena by looking for patterns in data. The

---

1. Students use science and engineering practices (SEPs) and crosscutting concept (CCs) to learn about magnets. They "plan and conduct an investigation collaboratively to produce data to serve as the basis for evidence" (NGSS Lead States 2013, p. 55). Their experiences highlight a CC used in science that "patterns can be used as evidence to support an explanation" (NGSS Lead States 2013, p. 92).

whole-group discussion was a bridge to developing a deeper understanding of magnetic properties during the Elaborate phase.[2]

Elaborate

My goal for the Elaborate phase was to have students develop a deeper and broader understanding of magnets. I engaged students in the first portion of this phase by showing them the materials they would use—two bar magnets (with north and south poles marked) and a compass. First, I asked students to tie a string around the middle of one bar magnet and hang it so the magnet could swing freely. Students used the other bar magnet to investigate the relationship between the magnetic poles of the two bar magnets. The students noticed that when they moved a bar magnet next to the magnet hanging freely by a string, they could make the hanging magnet move in a circle. The students also noticed that they could make the two magnets attract each other. As a result, they learned that similar poles of bar magnets repel each other, but opposite sides of bar magnets attract.

Next, students slowly moved a compass around one bar magnet. To their surprise, the compass needle moved in a full circle as they slowly moved the compass all the way around the bar magnet. The students inferred from the first investigation that the compass needle, like a bar magnet, had a north and a south pole. From these experiences, they discovered two important properties of magnets: (1) Like poles of magnets repel each other and unlike poles of magnets attract each other, and (2) the magnetic forces are strongest at the poles of the bar magnets.[3]

I introduced the second portion of the Elaborate phase with a challenge: "Which of three different sizes of magnets (one large, one medium, one small and horseshoe shaped) will hold the largest number of paper clips?" After students had time to think, I elicited their ideas; most thought the largest magnet would hold the most paper clips. The students worked in pairs to test the strength of the three different sizes of magnets. The medium-sized magnet was the strongest of the three magnets, and the activity quickly became a competition to see which team of students could hang the most paper clips from it. Thus, students inferred that the strength of a magnet is not dependent on the magnet's size. Investigating important factors in different types of

---

2. Students use many SEPs that are interconnected. They "analyze and interpret data to make sense of phenomena, using logical reasoning, mathematics, and/or computation" (NGSS Lead States 2013, p. 57). Students' experiences with data allow them to "use evidence (e.g., measurements, observations, patterns) to construct or support an explanation or design a solution to a problem" (NGSS Lead States 2013, p. 61). Their experiences allow them to "ask questions that can be investigated and predict reasonable outcomes based on patterns such as cause and effect relationships" (NGSS Lead States 2013, p. 51). Their new questions start the SEP cycle over again. Once they have a deeper understanding, students "communicate scientific and/or technical information orally and/or in written formats, including various forms of media as well as tables, diagrams, and charts" (NGSS Lead States 2013, p. 65).

3. Students continue to use SEPs during the Elaborate phase and "analyze and interpret data to make sense of phenomena, using logical reasoning, mathematics, and/or computation" (NGSS Lead States 2013, p. 57). Students' data analysis leads them to "use evidence (e.g., measurements, observations, patterns) to construct or support an explanation or design a solution to a problem" (NGSS Lead States 2013, p. 61).

interactions is an important physical science learning goal and could be extended to other explorations.

Evaluate

My goal for the Evaluate phase was for students to assess their understanding of the properties of magnets in a new and different situation. To accomplish this, I had the students complete a summative evaluation. In addition to answering selected response-type test questions, students answered a critical-response item concerning a demonstration I performed. I showed the students five magnetic rings. Next, I slid the magnetic rings onto an acrylic rod that was mounted on a base. To the students' amazement, when I let go of the magnetic rings, they floated with a small amount of air between each ring. Based on their experiences in this lesson, students were able to explain that the ring magnets are arranged so their like poles face each other; hence, the magnets repel each other.

Because of students' firsthand experiences, they learned a lot about magnets and addressed the three dimensions of the *NGSS* (see the *NGSS* connections in Table 8.4).

Table 8.4. *Unwrapping the Standards in Chapter 8*

Motion and Stability: Forces and Interactions	Connections to Classroom Activity
Performance Expectations	
3-PS2-3: Ask questions to determine cause and effect relationships of electric or magnetic interactions between two objects not in contact with each other. **3-PS2-4:** Define a simple design problem that can be solved by applying scientific ideas about magnets.	Students conduct experiments on different phenomena related to the properties of magnetic materials and magnetic forces. Students use their understanding of magnetic forces to solve a problem involving floating magnets.
Science and Engineering Practices	
Asking questions and defining problems	Students make predictions about materials in the science classroom that are magnetic or not magnetic. In addition, students make predictions about whether magnetic forces can act through different objects as the material between the objects changes and the distance between materials changes.
Analyzing and interpreting data	Students use data from observations to list magnetic versus nonmagnetic materials and examine how different factors influence magnetic forces.
Planning and carrying out investigations	Students carry out investigations to learn whether materials are magnetic or not and how two magnets interact when placed in contact with each other.
Constructing explanations and designing solutions	Students formulate evidence-based claim statements about magnetic properties and forces.
Obtaining, evaluating, and communicating information	Students share their knowledge of magnetic properties with their peers.
Disciplinary Core Idea	
PS2.B: Types of Interactions: Electric, and magnetic forces between a pair of objects do not require that the objects be in contact. The sizes of the forces in each situation depend on the properties of the objects and their distances apart and, for forces between two magnets, on their orientation relative to each other.	Students learn that magnetic forces relate to the distance between objects. As the distance increases, magnetic forces decrease, and vice versa. In addition, students learn that magnetic forces can act through different mediums such as some gases (air), liquids (water), and solids (tabletop). In addition, students learn that nonmetal materials are not magnetic and that only some metal materials in the classroom are magnetic (iron-containing materials).
Crosscutting Concept	
Patterns	Students work together to look for patterns among magnets and materials in the classroom.

Note: The materials, lessons, and activities outlined in this chapter are just one step toward reaching the performance expectations listed in this table. Additional supporting materials, lessons, and activities will be required. See *www.nextgenscience. org/msps-e-energy* for more information.

Chapter 9

Making the Connection: Addressing Students' Misconceptions of Circuits

Chapter 9

Explanations that stick or remain with students throughout a course happen when students play a major role in forming scientific claims. In this chapter, elementary students explore phenomena related to understanding the question "Why do the lights turn on when we flip the switch?" Electricity is an abstract phenomenon that students interact with every day.

This "batteries and bulbs" lesson, structured by the 5E Instructional Model, helps students build on their prior ideas with new experiences and understanding and seamlessly integrates all dimensions of *A Framework for K–12 Science Education* (National Research Council 2012). This chapter focuses on the lesson-level performance expectations, and students ask questions about data to understand how electrical circuits work and to explore how energy is transferred in an electrical circuit, along with the factors influencing the strength of electric forces.

Engage

Teachers can begin their unit on circuits by engaging students in a problem-based scenario that addresses scientifically oriented questions. This is a simple way to elicit students' prior knowledge about circuit setup and motivates them with a problem set in a real-life context. I begin by passing out the problem scenario to students:

> *Finally, the tent is set up, wood has been gathered for the campfire, and the camp cookout will begin in less than two hours. It is the perfect time for a quick hike into the woods before dusk. In a hurry, you grab the essentials: one flashlight, a sandwich, and your hiking stick. Dark settles in much sooner than anticipated, and the path of the trail is becoming harder to see. Luckily, you have your old, trusty flashlight to help you get back. You hit the switch, but nothing happens. Quickly, you unscrew the battery cap. Yikes, it only has one battery and needs two! Before panic sets in, you take a seat on a rock to think through the situation. The flashlight has one small light bulb; one small, transparent plastic piece to protect the bulb; one battery; and some wires housed in its plastic shell. You also have a sandwich wrapped in aluminum foil. Your walking stick is made of wood. How can you use what you know about circuits to light the bulb and make it back to camp safely?*

Each student brainstorms the problem by writing or drawing out his or her ideas on a sheet of paper. After five minutes, the students get into groups of three or four and share their ideas with each other (see Figure 9.1).

Figure 9.1. *Student Predictions About How to Light a Bulb Using Wires, a Battery, and a Light Bulb*

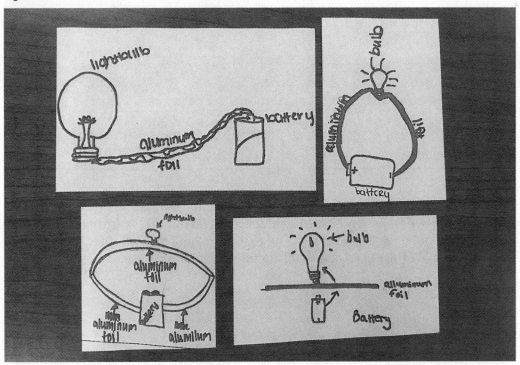

Chapter 9

Explore

The groups of three to four students are given a basket of materials. The basket contains a plastic flashlight, one battery, and a piece of aluminum foil. I tell the students, "You don't want to get lost in the woods. Get the light to work!"[1] They work in their groups using the materials and safety guidelines listed in Table 9.1.

Table 9.1. *Materials and Safety Considerations for Exploring Electrical Circuits*

Materials:
• Aluminum foil
• One AA battery
• One plastic flashlight that requires two batteries
• Three flashlight bulbs (plastic flashlights, which include the bulb, can be bought at several different department stores for $1.35–$1.75)

Safety:
• Wear sanitized, indirectly vented chemical splash safety goggles or safety glasses with side shields during the setup, hands-on, and take-down segments of the activity, for both students and teacher.
• Use caution when working with bulbs, wires, and so forth. They can cut or puncture skin!
• Use only nonrechargeable AA batteries. Do not use household or school electrical outlets.
• Use the specified materials only. Short circuits produced using a rechargeable nickel-cadmium cell will cause instant burns.
• Precautions should be taken when working with glass light bulbs and wire.
• Keep a charged fire extinguisher in the classroom. Fire precautions need to be taken when students explore electricity hands-on.
• Do not allow students to connect multiple batteries together to create a circuit.
• Have direct adult supervision when students are working with batteries and other electrical components.
• Wash your hands with soap and water after completing this activity.

The students first refer to their drawings to light the bulb. Often, to students' surprise, the bulb does not light. Once the students test their initial setup to see if the bulb does or does not work, they need to try other ways to light the bulb. I tell the groups to draw their successful and unsuccessful attempts. With time, students collect evidence

---

1. Students start their explorations with two related science and engineering practices (SEPs). They "define a simple design problem that can be solved through the development of an object, tool, process, or system and includes several criteria for success and constraints on materials, time, or cost" (NGSS Lead States 2013, p. 51). Their design solution will allow them to "make observations and/or measurements to produce data to serve as the basis for evidence for an explanation of a phenomenon or to test a design solution" (NGSS Lead States 2013, p. 55).

and figure out how to light the bulb, but they still do not know why it worked. Some students observe that when they hooked up the circuit, the battery terminals became hot, but the light did not glow. This is one observation that can be explored further. After 15 minutes of exploring ways to light the bulb, I tell the class to observe the wires in the flashlight bulb. As shown in Figure 9.2, the clear bulb allows students to make visual observations of the contact points inside the bulb.

Many students do not know that there are two contact points in a standard light bulb. These contact points or areas—the rivet and screw threads—must be in circuit. Each contact point must go to an opposite battery terminal. Students write down their questions and observations (e.g., "Where are the contact points in the bulb?") and then try again to light the bulb using the battery and aluminum foil they used earlier. The students' knowledge of the bulb's contact points results in success. Thus, students are using patterns in data to help develop understanding.[2]

Explain

The Explain phase is initiated with students' evidence-based claims. The students articulate in writing that the bulbs, wires, and batteries must form a complete loop from the negative terminal of the battery to the bulb and back to the positive terminal of the battery to light the bulb.[3] Students' claims are supported by evidence statements

Figure 9.2. *A Bulb Lighting Up Because It Is Part of a Complete Circuit*

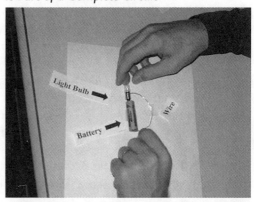

Figure 9.3. *An Incomplete Circuit Because the Wire Does Not Form a Complete Loop*

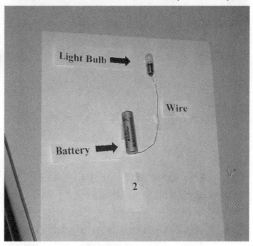

referencing battery-bulb-wire setups that worked or did not work during the Explore phase. Once the students have constructed an explanation, I support their developing understanding with a description and picture. I begin by drawing two circuits on the board. One circuit will not light because it does not form a complete electrical loop (see Figure 9.3), and the other one will. I ask, "Which circuit will light?"

---

2. Students use an SEP to extend learning, and they "compare and contrast data collected by different groups in order to discuss similarities and differences in their findings" (NGSS Lead States 2013, p. 57). The students' data analysis is evidence for a crosscutting concept used throughout the course and emphasizes that "patterns can be used as evidence to support an explanation" (NGSS Lead States 2013, p. 92).

3. Students' experiences with data and evidence straightforwardly connect to an SEP, and they "use evidence (e.g., measurements, observations, patterns) to construct or support an explanation or design a solution to a problem" (NGSS Lead States 2013, p. 61).

I follow this up by asking students "Why?" I call on them for their explanations. Then I ask, "Does anyone want to comment or have a question about this explanation?" I probe the class, asking for multiple explanations. After the students have argued their points, I simply tell the class to test their hypotheses. I draw on the board a circuit that relates the conflicting explanations. Students test their conflicting ideas with their group materials. After a thorough investigation of ideas, I introduce the class to the concept and requirements of a closed circuit. The light will glow when the first battery terminal is connected to the light's first contact point and the second battery terminal is connected to the light's second contact point. This allows the current to flow from one battery terminal to the bulb, out of the bulb, and to the second battery terminal.

Figure 9.4. *A Short Circuit Because the Wire Does Not Touch the Screw Threads*

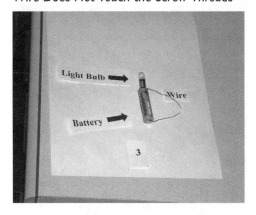

I extend the activity to other possible cases where batteries, wires, and bulbs are connected in sequence but do not form a complete electrical loop. Students frequently observe a short circuit when they think they have formed a complete electrical loop, yet they do not know why it occurs. A short circuit is observed when the battery terminals are connected through wire leads but the bulb is not connected in the circuit (see Figure 9.4). The current flows from the first battery terminal directly to the second battery terminal without traveling through the bulb.

The students revisit the initial activity of the lesson. For a second time, I ask them to draw a circuit that would make a bulb light using one battery, one bulb, and a piece of foil. I then ask them to compare and contrast this drawing with the first drawing they made at the start of the class. I ask the students, "How has your drawing of a closed circuit changed from when we started the lesson? Was your initial drawing a closed circuit, a short circuit, or an open circuit? Why has your drawing changed?" I collect their drawings and their explanations. After class, I read their explanations, investigating whether any individual is holding on to a misconception.

Elaborate

Once students have a basic understanding of forming simple series circuits, they develop a deeper understanding of current and resistance. The students build circuits with multiple bulbs and are challenged to create examples of situations that meet the following criteria: (1) When multiple bulbs are added and one light goes out, all lights go out; and (2) when multiple bulbs are added and one bulb goes out, the other bulbs stay on. The students make evidence-based claims about the two challenges. The elaboration challenges help them better understand the flow of electrical energy and resistance. For instance, students are able to make an evidence-based claim that when only one electrical pathway exists, adding bulbs (i.e., resistance) causes a decrease in the brightness of light produced. In addition, if one bulb is unscrewed and removed from the circuit, then all of the lights go out.

Conversely, in a multiple-pathway electrical circuit (i.e., parallel), there are multiple ways for electricity to get to the bulbs. Unscrewing one bulb from the circuit does not have an impact on whether the remaining bulbs stay lit. In addition, the brightness of light produced by all bulbs is the same. My goal for the elaboration activities was to get students to start to understand the different ways that electricity can flow and the impact of adding sources of electrical resistance in a circuit.

In addition to focusing on the similarities and differences between single- and multiple-pathway electrical circuits (i.e., series vs. parallel), we make connections to energy transformations. This lesson relates to students' prior learning experiences and represents an energy where the batteries contain chemical energy, the wires transfer electrical energy, and the light bulbs produce electromagnetic energy and some thermal energy. Thus, students' firsthand experiences provide them with a meaningful and relevant context for understanding energy transformations.

Evaluate

Like engineers and scientists, my students share their research on parallel circuits in a presentation to their peers. Students are always surprised by how many different ways they can create parallel circuits.[4] In addition to presentations, teachers can ask students to write a short report describing their overall conclusions about series and parallel circuits. I use students' pictures from their presentations as questions on their summative exam. I ask them to explain the brightness of bulbs and whether bulbs will remain lit when bulbs are added or "burn out" in various circuits. Students enjoy having their class examples on the end-of-unit test and can use their firsthand experiences to justify their answers to questions.

The end outcome of this lesson is that students learn about circuits through authentic experiences. This lesson also addresses the three dimensions of the *NGSS* (see Table 9.2, p. 94).

---

4. Students use many intertwined SEPs to gain a deeper understanding of electricity. First, they "compare and contrast data collected by different groups in order to discuss similarities and differences in their findings" (NGSS Lead States 2013, p. 57). Second, their data analysis allows them to "use evidence (e.g., measurements, observations, patterns) to construct or support an explanation or design a solution to a problem" (NGSS Lead States 2013, p. 61). Lastly, they "communicate scientific and/or technical information orally and/or in written formats, including various forms of media as well as tables, diagrams, and charts" (NGSS Lead States 2013, p. 65).

Chapter 9

Table 9.2. *Unwrapping the Standards in Chapter 9*

Energy	Connections to Classroom Activity
Performance Expectation	
4-PS3-2: Make observations to provide evidence that energy can be transferred from place to place by sound, light, heat, and electric currents.	Students conduct experiments on different types of electrical circuits to learn how energy is transferred.
Science and Engineering Practices	
Asking questions and defining problems	Students make predictions about how to light a bulb using foil, light bulbs, and batteries.
Analyzing and interpreting	Students use data from their observations to understand combinations of wires, bulbs, and batteries that will complete circuits.
Planning and carrying out investigations	Students carry out investigations to learn about series and parallel circuits.
Constructing explanations and designing solutions	Students formulate evidence-based claim statements about series and parallel circuits.
Obtaining, evaluating, and communicating information	Students share their knowledge of series and parallel circuits through a presentation to their peers.
Disciplinary Core Ideas	
PS3.A: Definitions of Energy: Energy can be moved from place to place by moving objects or through sound, light, or electric currents.	Students learn that in series circuits, charges pass through every light bulb.
PS3.B: Conservation of Energy and Energy Transfer: Energy can also be transferred from place to place by electric currents, which can then be used locally to produce motion, sound, heat, or light. The currents may have been produced to begin with by transforming the energy of motion into electrical energy.	Students' elaborations show them that the overall resistance for each bulb added increases when bulbs are added (current decreases). In addition, students explain that in parallel circuits, because there are multiple pathways for electricity to flow, the overall resistance decreases when bulbs are added (current increases).
Crosscutting Concepts	
Patterns	Students work together to look for patterns among the materials (wires, batteries, and bulbs).
Energy and matter: Flow, cycles, and conservation	Students also use the idea that energy transfers from one object to another but is never created or destroyed to think about the types of energy transfers in a circuit and conservation of energy.

Note: The materials, lessons, and activities outlined in this chapter are just one step toward reaching the performance expectation listed in this table. Additional supporting materials, lessons, and activities will be required. See *www.nextgenscience.org/msps-e-energy* for more information.

Chapter 10

Gliding Into Understanding

Chapter 10

In each of the model lessons presented thus far, highly effective instructional strategies help students learn science. These strategies include demonstrations, laboratory investigations, discussions, and mini-lectures. This chapter offers a 5E lesson with Elaborate and Evaluate phases that places students in the role of scientist and asks them to carry out "next-step" investigations. The next-step investigations challenge students to build on what they have learned during explorations and explanations and to apply it to deepen their understanding of important science process and content.

This 5E lesson appeals to students' interests and is directly related to the phenomenon of flight. Coming into the lesson, students hold incomplete views of the forces acting on objects in motion. Students who master this content can explain the following *NGSS* performance expectation: "Plan and conduct an investigation to provide evidence of the effects of balanced and unbalanced forces on the motion of an object" (3-PS2-1; NGSS Lead States 2013).

As they progress through the activities, students use nearly all of the *NGSS* scientific and engineering practices (see the footnote connections). In addition, the lesson includes many chances to bridge science content with the *Common Core State Standards for English Language Arts* (*CCSS ELA*) and the *Common Core State Standards for Mathematics* (*CCSS Math*) (National Governors Association Center for Best Practices and Council of Chief State School Officers [NGAC and CCSSO] 2010). Because of the combined 5E and *NGSS* focus in the paper airplane activity, students develop deeper conceptual understandings and a greater ability to perform controlled science experiments for the remainder of the school year.

Engage (one 60-minute class period)

The engagement phase is a chance to elicit students' prior knowledge and experiences and motivate them to learn science. When my students entered the classroom, I challenged them to work in groups of three to create a paper airplane using a half sheet of paper. The students predicted how far in centimeters their paper airplane would fly and described the forces acting on a paper airplane in flight based on their experiences in earlier grades. I emphasized that although students may want to test their ideas, they should not throw their paper planes at this point.

The students' predictions lent insight to their knowledge of metric units. Some students thought the paper airplanes would fly only 10 cm, while others thought the planes would fly 100 m. In addition, their ideas about forces acting on a paper airplane in flight revealed their knowledge of force and motion. Students' predictions are formative assessments and inform the design of subsequent activities.

SAFETY NOTES

1. Wear sanitized, indirectly vented chemical splash safety goggles or safety glasses with side shields during the setup, hands-on, and take-down segments of the activity, for both students and teacher.
2. Fly airplanes only in an established fly zone. Ensure that there are no fragile items in the zone.
3. Have direct adult supervision when constructing and flying planes.
4. Use caution when working with sharp objects (e.g., scissors) in constructing the plane. They can cut skin.
5. Wash your hands with soap and water after completing this activity.

Explore (two 60-minute class periods)

Once students have had a chance to work together, I facilitate discussions to help them explore paper airplanes. First, I ask students to think of an investigative question given the available materials and directions they have received so far. We use students' predictions and the paper airplanes created so far to help us formalize

Chapter 10

our research question. My students noticed that there were many different predictions and three main types of paper airplanes created, identifiable by the nose design: "dart," "normal," and "glider" (see Figure 10.1).

Figure 10.1. *Three Types of Paper Airplanes*

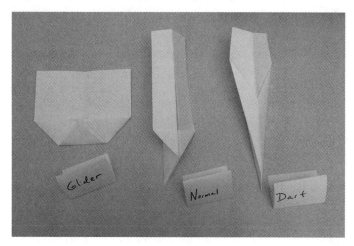

By focusing on the materials they could test and what they had already done (made a paper airplane), the students decided as a class to investigate the question "Does the style of paper airplane (dart vs. normal vs. glider) influence how far it travels?"[1] The students were now eager to test their planes; however, it is beneficial to discuss with students some science content behind airplane flight to develop a basic theoretical understanding and to ensure that the tests are reasonably accurate. The discussions about science content and experimental procedures are a good way to (formatively) assess students' content knowledge and thoughts about experimental design.

We started by constructing a list of forces acting upon a paper airplane in flight (see Figure 10.2). I called on volunteers to share their ideas. Most students realized that a paper airplane has an applied force (from the thrower). Some students mentioned that the force of gravity pulls the airplane down toward the ground. Few students identified air resistance as a force, and no students mentioned lift forces exerted by the airplane on the surrounding air (i.e., normal force). The students could use their models to explain the direction a paper airplane would fly and make predictions about how changing the direction of a force could influence flight.

Figure 10.2. *Forces Acting on Paper Airplanes*

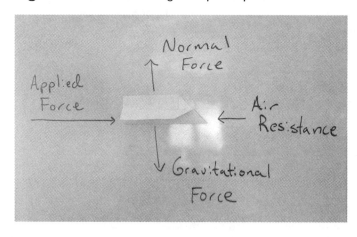

The next part of the class focused on what we called fair-test issues to ensure that when the students conducted the experiment, they used standard data

---

1. Students start the Explore phase with a science and engineering practice (SEP) and "ask questions about what would happen if a variable is changed" (NGSS Lead States 2013, p. 51).

NATIONAL SCIENCE TEACHING ASSOCIATION

collection procedures and followed safety practices. Generating a list of fair-test issues and a scientific procedure addresses the *CCSS ELA*, as students have to design "steps for a technical procedure" (CCSS.ELA-Literacy.RI.3.3; NGAC and CCSSO 2010). As a class, the students generated a list of fair-test issues and safety guidelines (see Table 10.1).[2]

Table 10.1. *Fair-Test Issues and Safety Guidelines for Conducting Investigations Using Paper Airplanes*

1. Have one partner mark where the plane lands.
2. Note that the distance traveled is the point where the plane hits the ground.
3. Redo flights when the plane's flight is disrupted (it hits a table or wall).
4. Throw the plane from approximately 2.5 m high.
5. Conduct three trials.
6. Do not disrupt other people's planes.
7. Wear protective eyewear when conducting the experiment.
8. When not performing data collection trials, sit by the wall in the gymnasium out of the way of the testing corridors.

I let students take turns presenting ideas as I wrote them on large poster paper for everyone to see. The result of the discussions was that the students developed ownership for learning because they played an active role in generating the exploration. Once the students had developed the investigation, they explored the relationship between the paper airplane style and the distance the airplanes travel.[3] They worked in groups of three, and each group tested all three types of paper airplanes. Each group of students constructed the paper airplanes. Each student was assigned a role—either "thrower," "measurer," or "data recorder"—and the students rotated roles each trial.

To help manage the class and to ensure that there was enough space, we tested the paper airplanes in the gymnasium. For safety reasons, we used masking tape to mark off testing corridors, so many different groups could test their paper airplanes at the same time. The students who were testing wore protective eyewear. When the students were not conducting trials, they cheered on their classmates and stayed out of the testing area by sitting against the gymnasium wall.

---

2. Students use many SEPs in concert, all aimed at helping them develop understanding. Students "develop and/ or use models to describe and/or predict phenomena" (NGSS Lead States 2013, p. 53). In addition, they "plan and conduct an investigation collaboratively to produce data to serve as the basis for evidence, using fair tests in which variables are controlled and the number of trials is considered" (NGSS Lead States 2013, p. 55).

3. Students' experimental designs lead directly to an SEP, and they "make observations and/or measurements to produce data to serve as the basis for evidence for an explanation of a phenomenon or to test a design solution" (NGSS Lead States 2013, p. 55).

Chapter 10

Explain (two 60-minute class periods)

The first portion of the concept explanation phase was dedicated to compiling data and making scientific claims based on evidence. I put up a data chart on the board with spaces to list paper airplane style, trials, total, and mean. The students copied the table onto their own pieces of paper and worked with their groups to fill in the chart with their data (see Table 10.2).

Table 10.2. *Student Predictions and Data Table for Paper Airplane Investigation*

Style of Paper Airplane	Distance Traveled (cm)					
	Prediction	*Trial 1*	*Trial 2*	*Trial 3*	*Total*	*Mean*
Dart	100	750	727	773	2,250	750
Glider	50	115	107	105	327	109
Normal	90	435	423	400	1,258	419.33

They then worked together to analyze the data, looking for patterns between the mean distance traveled and the style of the paper airplane. I assessed the students' abilities to calculate totals and means (including units) and provided feedback so they could accurately perform these calculations in subsequent activities.

Next, I asked questions to help students make sense of the data. For instance, I asked them to look at the highest mean numbers and the lowest mean numbers to determine whether there was a relationship between distance traveled and the style of paper airplane. This activity required them to use the *Common Core State Standards for Mathematics* practice of using quantitative data to reason abstractly (CCSS.Math.Practice.MP.2; NGAC and CCSSO 2010). The students quickly noticed that the dart-style paper airplanes consistently flew farther than the normal or glider paper airplanes. Once they made a claim based on evidence, they engaged in conversations concerning why certain paper airplanes fly farther than others. I encouraged the students to present ideas, ask questions, and justify claims based on evidence when they were discussing paper airplane flight (CCSS.ELA-Literacy.SL3.1; NGAC and CCSSO 2010).

My students generated a flurry of ideas. One student said, "Darts flew the farthest because they are more aerodynamic." You may find that students use the term *aerodynamic* without understanding how the shape of an airplane and an air resistance force influence paper airplane flight. I asked the students to think about the differences among the paper airplanes using force diagrams. They realized that the force of air resistance is greater for glide and normal paper airplanes, which have greater frontal surface area, than for dart-style paper airplanes.[4] I also introduced the students to the idea that the size of the arrow illustrates the magnitude of a force. They had little trouble comprehending that larger throwing forces are depicted by longer arrows.

Finally, the students discussed whether an object that is not moving has forces acting on it. They realized that when objects are not in motion, the sum of the forces is zero—not that there is no force acting on the object. My students demonstrated this understanding with their explanation that gravity is always acting on an object; therefore, other forces must also be acting that are equal in size and opposite in direction. The explanation discussion engages students in generating reasoning for their thinking—skills that they will use during the remainder of the year when conducting more open-ended inquiries.

Once the students have provided explanations for their investigations and discussions with fundamental science practices, I introduce formal science terminology in light of their experiences. For example, I introduce the term *independent variable* (manipulated) to refer to the factor purposely changed and the term *dependent variable* (responding) to indicate the factor measured and reported as the result.

During the Explain phase, students also investigated scientific conclusions. They were provided with three different scientific conclusions and considered their attributes to derive a common set of guidelines for writing their own conclusions. For example, one sample conclusion statement had a misspelling, provided the research question, and answered the investigative question but did not offer data or evidence. The second conclusion had an incomplete sentence and provided a research question and data to support a claim but made no scientific claim. The students learned that a well-written conclusion identifies the problem being investigated, generates a scientific claim based on data and evidence, and states the relationship between the variables in an experiment.

Thus, the students learned that a scientific conclusion is a specialized way of writing a summary of the most significant findings and the relationship between variables in an experiment (CCSS.ELA-Literacy.RIL3.3; NGAC and CCSSO 2010). As a result of the concept explanation phase, the students derived knowledge of formal terminology and concepts through firsthand involvement with data, prior experiences, examples, and discussions with the teacher.

Elaborate (three 60-minute class periods)

The aim of the Elaborate phase is for students to apply new ideas in similar contexts. The students work in their groups of three to design a "next-step" investigation. The

---

4. Students use three SEPs in tandem that lend support for a reoccurring crosscutting concept (CC). First, they "analyze and interpret data to make sense of phenomena, using logical reasoning, mathematics, and/ or computation" (NGSS Lead States 2013, p. 57). Their data lead directly to students "applying simple data sets to reveal patterns that suggest relationships" (NGSS Lead States 2013, p. 59). Finally, they "use evidence (e.g., measurements, observations, patterns) to construct or support an explanation or design a solution to a problem" (NGSS Lead States 2013, p. 61). Students' experiences lend evidence to a CC in the course, where "patterns can be used as evidence to support an explanation" (NGSS Lead States 2013, p. 92).

next-step investigation required the students to design a new and different scientific research question to explore paper airplanes. They were instructed to change only one variable and to think about the factor they would measure and report on for the investigative results.

My students were very excited about the Elaborate phase and generated a flood of unique ideas. Some students wanted to test whether the size of the paper used to make paper airplanes influences the distance they travel. Others wanted to know whether the type of paper (construction, card stock, computer, or lined paper) used to make the planes influences the distance they travel. Several students tested whether changing mass by using paper clips affects airplane flight. A few students wanted to know whether paper airplanes travel farther outside or inside.[5]

Once the students decided on a research question as a group, they carried out their investigation in the gymnasium and wrote up lab reports, including the procedure followed, data tables and graphs, force diagrams (models for the forces acting on a paper airplane according to the data collected), and conclusions.[6] This investigation was a great way for students to build and elaborate on their knowledge—an essential skill—of forces and motion (CCSSW.3.7; NGAC and CCSSO 2010). I aimed to provide the students with investigative time and to ask probing questions to make sure that they changed only one factor in their investigation (summative assessment).

Evaluate (one 60-minute class period)

Like scientists, the students gave brief, five-minute presentations that described their next-step research questions and main findings.[7] The next-step laboratory write-up and presentation was the culminating activity for the unit and the summative assessment of the students' understanding of scientific practices. In addition, the lab write-up is a way for students to "examine a topic and convey ideas, concepts, and information through the selection, organization, and analysis of relevant content" (NGAC and CCSSO 2010, p. 42). I checked each component of the students' projects. I graded their data tables and graphs for accuracy and checked their diagrams to make sure their force diagrams included gravity and allied forces. In addition, I assessed the students' written conclusions to ensure that they provided the following: (1) a summary of their investigation, (2) data for the highs and lows, and (3) a statement describing the relationship between the independent and dependent variables in their investigation. The students enjoyed presenting their unique investigations and were proud of their work as scientists.

---

5. Students' experiences with data and evidence lead to an SEP, and they "ask questions about what would happen if a variable is changed" (NGSS Lead States 2013, p. 51).

6. Students use an SEP and "plan and conduct an investigation collaboratively to produce data to serve as the basis for evidence, using fair tests in which variables are controlled and the number of trials is considered" (NGSS Lead States 2013, p. 55).

7. Students' final products require them to use an SEP, and they "communicate scientific and/or technical information orally and/or in written formats, including various forms of media as well as tables, diagrams, and charts" (NGSS Lead States 2013, p. 65).

Conclusions

This type of investigation captures students' attention, unveils knowledge about the science process, and incorporates the three dimensions of the *NGSS* (see *NGSS* connections in Table 10.3). The paper airplane investigation helped my students better conceptualize the parts of a scientific investigation when they compared the whole-class paper airplane activity with their "next-step" investigation. In addition, the paper airplane investigation helps students understand that only one variable can be manipulated in a controlled experiment to draw conclusive claims based on evidence. The students realized that they can change only the style of the paper airplane in the first investigation, and only one factor in their next-step experiment, in order to make valid scientific claims based on evidence (American Association for the Advancement of Science and Project 2061, n.d.).

Table 10.3. *Unwrapping the Standards in Chapter 10*

Motion and Stability: Forces and Interactions	Connections to Classroom Activity
Performance Expectations	
3-PS2-1: Plan and conduct an investigation to provide evidence of the effects of balanced and unbalanced forces on the motion of an object. **3-PS2-2:** Make observations and/or measurements of an object's motion to provide evidence that a pattern can be used to predict future motion.	Students work in groups to plan and carry out science investigations dealing with forces and interactions.
Science and Engineering Practices	
Asking questions and defining problems	Students investigate whether the style of paper airplane (dart vs. normal vs. glider) influences how far it travels.
Analyzing and interpreting data	Students look for patterns in data to make claims about the relationship between the style of the paper airplane and its flight.
Developing and using models	Students learn how to use force diagrams as a model for describing how many different forces interact and whether the interaction among forces results in motion.
Planning and carrying out investigations	Students develop a list of fair-test issues to ensure that when they conduct experiments, they use similar data collection and safety procedures. Once students conduct experiments, they work together to analyze the data.
Using mathematics and computational thinking	Students calculate means from raw data to look for patterns.

Continued

Table 10.3. (*continued*)

Motion and Stability: Forces and Interactions	Connections to Classroom Activity
Science and Engineering Practices (*continued*)	
Obtaining, evaluating, and communicating information	Students' paper airplane conclusions make a scientific claim based on evidence they have obtained firsthand.
Disciplinary Core Ideas	
PS2.A: Forces and Motion: Each force acts on one particular object and has both strength and a direction. An object at rest typically has multiple forces acting on it, but they add to give zero net force on the object. Forces that do not sum to zero can cause changes in the object's speed or direction of motion. (Boundary: Qualitative and conceptual, but not quantitative addition of forces are used at this level.)	Students learn that the sum of the forces acting on an object is related to the object's motion. When objects are not in motion, the sum of the forces is zero. Conversely, when the sum of forces is not equal to zero, the object moves in the direction of the predominating force(s). Students learned about different forces influencing flight, including applied force from the thrower, force of gravity, and air resistance.
PS2.A: Forces and Motion: The patterns of an object's motion in various situations can be observed and measured; when that past motion exhibits a regular pattern, future motion can be predicted from it. (Boundary: Technical terms, such as magnitude, velocity, momentum, and vector quantity, are not introduced at this level, but the concept that some quantities need both size and direction to be described is developed.)	Students make predictions based on their data about the distance an airplane will travel that are related to the airplane's design. Students use patterns in evidence to motivate their next-step investigations.
PS2.A: Forces and Motion: All positions of objects and the directions of forces and motions must be described in an arbitrarily chosen reference frame and arbitrarily chosen units of size. To share information with other people, these choices must also be shared.	Students learn that forces can be represented with arrows indicating size and direction.
Crosscutting Concept	
Patterns	Students work together to analyze data, looking for patterns between the mean distance traveled and the style of paper airplanes.

Note: The materials, lessons, and activities outlined in this chapter are just one step toward reaching the performance expectations listed in this table. Additional supporting materials, lessons, and activities will be required. See *www.nextgenscience.org/msps-e-energy* for more information.

Chapter 11

Is It a Change?

Chapter 11

Activity Box:
Using Assessment Probes to Determine
Prior Knowledge

1. Make an inventory of assessment probes that you currently use with students to address their prior knowledge and experiences.

2. Identify whether the assessment probe can directly translate to a firsthand experience with data.

3. Begin developing an assessment probe for *explore-before-explain* lessons by completing the following: (a) Identify how the assessment probe relates to a science phenomenon and is relevant and meaningful for students; (b) list the materials you will need for students to have *explore-before-explain* experiences; (c) decide whether any procedural explanations (not content) are necessary so that students know how science will be investigated; and (d) list the terms and ideas that will help sophisticate student understanding in light of the experiences.

4. Use the footnote connections provided in this chapter to interpret the details of how the *Next Generation Science Standards* (*NGSS*) can look in practice.

The connection between activities in this chapter's lesson—"Is It a Change?"— highlights the pivotal role that instructional sequence plays for learners. The sequence of assessing prior knowledge using tools that situate learning and directly lend themselves to explorations is a way to make science relevant. Next, simple shifts in the arrangement of hands-on activities at the beginning of new units of study can make a big difference for learners. Allowing students to first construct conceptual knowledge through firsthand experiences and articulate their understanding through evidence-based claims before developing ideas through explanations is paramount to an *explore-before-explain* approach. In this way, new knowledge is deeply entrenched in their firsthand experiences.

My fifth-grade lesson took two 50-minute class periods and targeted two interrelated performance expectations: (1) that students can "measure and graph quantities to provide evidence that regardless of the type of change that occurs when heating, cooling, or mixing substances, the total weight of matter is conserved" (5-PS1-2); and (2) that they can "conduct an investigation to determine whether the mixing of two or more substances results in new substances" (5-PS1-4; NGSS Lead States 2013). These activities help confront student misconceptions about chemical reactions and that matter can disappear (see Driver et al. 1994). In grades 3–5, students can recognize when substances change form; however, they have difficulty understanding that the parts of materials change their form during a chemical reaction or change. Although the chemical details are sophisticated, students can compare and contrast the amount of materials and their form before and after a chemical reaction. They can construct conceptual ideas about chemical changes creating new and different materials.

This lesson is one step in helping students develop an understanding of the conservation of matter that takes place during a chemical change, and it addresses all three dimensions of the *NGSS* (see the *NGSS* connections table at the end of the chapter). This *explore-before-explain* lesson includes a prior knowledge assessment probe, a demonstration, students' evidence-based claims, and an explanation from the teacher.

The Assessment Probe

The students were engaged in an assessment probe ("Is It a Change?") that directly addresses misconceptions and lends itself to firsthand investigations. In this way, the assessment probe both situates learning about phenomena associated with specific content (disciplinary core ideas) and highlights the role that asking questions, testing predictions, and carrying out investigations plays in science learning (science and engineering practices). I read the "Is It a Change?" assessment probe out loud to the class (*see next page*).

Is It a Change?

You are having an argument with your friend about what happens when you mix vinegar and baking soda.

Predict what will happen when you mix vinegar and baking soda below.

Before	After

1. **Which of the following best describes the results of the material's masses? Circle your prediction.**
   a. The mass of the materials will be more before the reaction takes place.
   b. The mass of the materials will be more after the reaction takes place.
   c. The mass of the materials will be the same before and after the reaction.

2. **Which of the following best describes the results of the material's temperatures? Circle your prediction.**
   a. The temperature of the materials will be higher before the reaction takes place.
   b. The temperature of the materials will be higher after the reaction takes place.
   c. The temperatures of the materials will be the same before and after the reaction.

3. **Where did your ideas come from? Circle all that apply.**
   a. A book I read
   b. A movie or television show
   c. Talking with my friends or family
   d. Websites or videos
   e. Social media
   f. Posters or other pictures
   g. My own experience
   h. Other people's experiences
   i. Things we did in class this year
   j. Things we did in other classes
   k. Logic—it makes sense to me
   l. Evidence from observation

The students made predictions about what they thought baking soda and vinegar would look like before and after they were combined. I showed them two beakers, one with 50 ml of vinegar and the other with 50 ml of baking soda. The students had a variety of ideas about what the substances would look like and what they would do when mixed. Many students thought the solution would "erupt" like a volcano (see Figures 11.1 and 11.2). Other students thought that the baking soda would dissolve in the vinegar.

Figure 11.1. *Student Prediction About "Is It a Change?"*

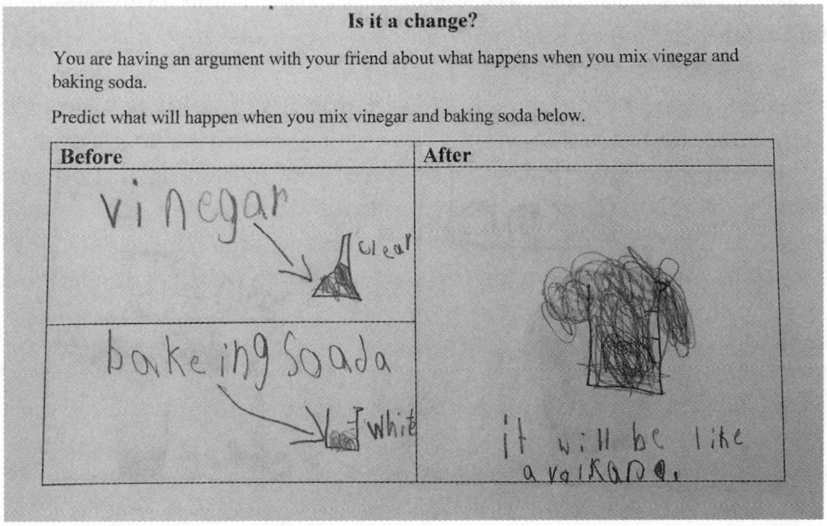

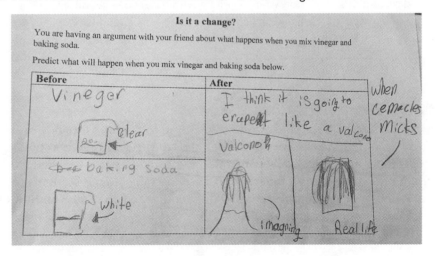

Figure 11.2. *Another Student Prediction About "Is It a Change?"*

Chapter 11

I had two follow-up content questions for the students that dealt with changes that may occur. The first was about changes in the mass of the materials and the second considered a change in temperature. The students had a range of ideas. Approximately half of the students thought that mass would be higher before the reaction. No students thought the mass would be the same. Students' ideas about change in temperature were also mixed. Fifty percent of students thought that the temperature would be higher after the baking soda and vinegar were mixed. Twenty-five percent thought that the temperature would be higher before the two materials were mixed. Finally, 25% thought the temperature would be the same before and after the materials were combined. The last question asked students to give some thought as to why they held certain conceptions (see Keeley 2019). Most students' responses were related to their past lived experiences (items *g*, *h*, *i*, and *j*).

The formative assessment data lend fascinating insights for teachers. Many students said that they had seen this demonstration or something like it before in a different class. Interestingly, while students may have seen the demonstration before, their mixed conceptions made me think that their prior knowledge did not provide them with experiences that promote long-lasting understanding. Thus, this was a ripe area for investigations, and my plan was for students to construct knowledge based on evidence they collect.

SAFETY NOTES

1. Wear sanitized, indirectly vented chemical splash safety goggles, nonlatex nitrile gloves, and a nonlatex apron during the setup, hands-on, and take-down segments of the activity, for both students and teacher.
2. Use caution when working with sharp objects (e.g., glassware). They can cut or puncture skin.
3. Have direct adult supervision when working with hazardous chemicals.
4. Immediately wipe up any liquid spilled on the floor—a slip-and-fall hazard.
5. Wash your hands with soap and water after completing this activity.

Hands-On Demonstrations

Once everyone had made a prediction, it was time to conduct a hands-on test. This "doing" of science requires a safe experience, and sanitized, indirectly vented chemical splash goggles are a requirement. I performed the demonstration and had students sit approximately 2.5 meters from the front observation table. Many students found that the initial demonstration confirmed their predictions and that the solution bubbled (see Figure 11.3).

While not as dramatic as they had hoped for (no "eruption"), the demonstration helped us conduct more rigorous investigations of the cause-and-effect relationship that was evident in the chemical reaction.[1] We considered the questions "When we mixed baking soda and vinegar into a single solution, did we create a new and different substance?" and "What evidence do we have to support our ideas?"[2] We talked about the before-and-after substances in terms of states of matter. The students explained that we mixed a solid (baking soda) to create a liquid and a gas. The bubbling and the production of gas were an excellent way to target the crosscutting concept of cause and effect and provided some beginning evidence that the solution had new and

Figure 11.3. *Students' Observations About What Happens When Vinegar and Baking Soda Are Mixed*

different properties (one being the production of a gas). At this point, we questioned whether a gas has mass and how we could measure it in an investigation. While the initial demonstration was anticlimactic, the conversation that followed intrigued students about the changes that would occur.

To delve into the variables from our formative assessment probe (mass and temperature), we needed to conduct further testing. To investigate changes in mass, I put 50 ml of vinegar in an Erlenmeyer flask. Next, I put baking soda in a nonlatex balloon. I carefully put the balloon on the Erlenmeyer flask, making sure not to mix the baking soda and the vinegar. I used some black electrical tape to seal the balloon to the Erlenmeyer flask and made sure there were little to no gaps (see the YouTube video at *https:// youtu.be/uxTsPLgFyo0* for the investigative setup). Finally, I placed the flask-balloon setup on an electronic balance. When teachers lift the balloon and gently shake the baking soda out of the balloon and into the vinegar, they initiate the chemical reaction. (*Note to teachers:* This demonstration is challenging to set up and mimics a closed system. Teachers should perform the demonstration beforehand because if the system is not as closed as possible, gas will be released, promoting misconceptions about the conservation of mass.)

We performed the demonstration on the electronic balance. (*As a cautionary note,* teachers should continue to wear sanitized, indirectly vented chemical safety protective goggles as well as a heavy-duty apron and gloves.) To many students' surprise,

1. Students' observations produce data to serve as the basis for evidence (NGSS Lead States 2013, p. 7).

2. Students' predictions help them "identify scientific (testable) and non-scientific (non-testable) questions" (NGSS Lead States 2013, p. 4).

Chapter 11

Figure 11.4. *A Student's Observations: (Top Section) Data About Mass From the Flask-Balloon Setup; (Middle Section) Temperature Data Before and After a Chemical Change; (Bottom Section) An Evidence-Based Claim*

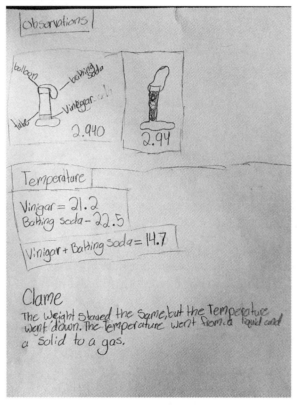

while the nonlatex balloon inflated, the mass did not change (the mass remained 2.940 g). See Figure 11.4, top section.[3]

The data highlighted the importance of the decimal places in this measurement, and each of the numbers, before and after the decimal, was important evidence needed to help us formulate our claim. The focus on the crosscutting concept of scale, proportion, and quantity was a nice bridge to the *Common Core State Standards for Mathematics* (*CCSS Math*), which emphasize that students gain abilities to represent a "data set of measurements in fractions of a unit" (CCSS.Math.Content.5.MD.B.2; National Governors Association Center for Best Practices and Council of Chief State School Officers [NGAC and CCSSO] 2010).[4]

The next demonstration was designed to test whether a change in temperature occurs during a chemical reaction. Equivalent amounts of baking soda and vinegar were placed in beakers. (We used 64.6 g as our equivalent amounts. While typically you would use a volume to measure a liquid, having equivalent masses was an easy way to illustrate that we were using the same amounts of substances. Any equivalent amounts would work for this demonstration.) Next, the temperature was taken of each element and the solution. The baking soda was 22.5°C and the vinegar was 21.2°C. The two materials had slightly different temperatures. When the materials were mixed, to students' surprise, the temperature decreased significantly, to 14.5°C.[5] See Figure 11.4, middle section.

---

3. Students "analyze and interpret data to make sense of phenomena" (NGSS Lead States 2013, p. 9).

4. Students use data to begin to understand that "observable phenomena exist from the very small to the immensely large" (NGSS Lead States 2013, p. 7).

5. Students use mathematical and computational thinking to describe the results of the demonstration (NGSS Lead States 2013).

Evidence-Based Claims

At this point in the lesson, I wanted students to articulate their understanding through writing. I pushed them to think about why conservation of mass occurs during chemical reactions in a closed system. As a class, we all had the same evidence related to phenomena. I asked the students to make a claims-evidence-reasoning (C-E-R) statement, to encourage them to construct explanations for phenomena. The first part of the students' C-E-R statement was aimed at explaining just the claim they could construct based on evidence they witnessed firsthand. In this regard, students' claims typically represent what they can explain on a conceptual level about science. One student wrote, "The weight stayed the same, but the temperature went down."

I also challenged the students to write a reasoning statement for why what they observed happened. To help guide them with the reasoning statement, I used a sentence frame so they would know how to engage in technical writing. I wrote on the board, "I think the weight staying the same had something to do with _____," and "The temperature decreasing when the two substances are mixed had something to do with _____." Students had very similar ideas for both of their reasoning statements. One student thought the mass remained the same because "the materials were all still there but just in a different form." For the second sentence frame, a student described that "the temperature decreased because the materials went from solids and liquids to some gas." For an example of a student evidence-based claim, see Figure 11.4, bottom section.

I was pleased with my students' reasoning statements at this point and decided that it was time to provide more elaborate explanations.

Authoritative Explanations

An authoritative explanation allows students to build on their prior experiences and knowledge by providing accurate content from a reliable source. To provide the students with an authoritative explanation, we read a short excerpt from a grade 3–4 reader titled *The Scoop About Measuring Matter*:

> Mass stays the same when an object changes physical properties, such as state, color, or shape.
>
> Mass also stays the same in a chemical reaction, when two combined materials change into entirely new material.
>
> ### The Law of Conservation of Mass
>
> In 1789, French chemist Antoine Lavoisier proved that mass put into a reaction equaled the mass that came out of the reaction. No new mass. No mass destroyed. Voilà, *you have the law of conservation of mass.* (Maurer 2013, pp. 16–17)

Thus, students formed a more elaborate understanding that the mass is conserved in a chemical reaction and this property is termed the "law of conservation of mass."

The teacher portion of the explanation dealt less with why the temperature decreased (the endothermic change goes beyond third- to fifth-grade content and is appropriate for high school) and focused on signs of chemical changes. In addition, the short reading verified students' firsthand experiences with an explanation from a credible source. For the class, I listed common indicators of chemical changes, which included the formation of gas bubbles, color change, and temperature change. The students decided as a class that because the temperature had changed during the reaction, a chemical reaction had occurred. Thus, the students inferred from the demonstration and temperature data that a new substance was produced that had different properties from baking soda and vinegar.

Once my students had a deeper understanding, I had them add to their reasoning statements. My goal was to wed students' firsthand experiences with data and authoritative explanations so that student construction of knowledge was elaborated to include more scientific understanding. The students' C-E-R statement was my summative evaluation of their learning and a way to bridge science with the *Common Core State Standards for English Language Arts* (*CCSS ELA*), which suggests that students "provide a concluding statement or section that follows from and supports the information or explanation presented" (CCSS.ELA-Literacy.W.5.1.D; NGAC and CCSSO 2010).

See Table 11.1 for the *NGSS* connections visited in this chapter.

Table 11.1. *Unwrapping the* Explore-Before-Explain *Chemical Change Investigation*

Matter and Its Interactions	Connections to Classroom Activity
Performance Expectations	
5-PS1-2: Measure and graph quantities to provide evidence that regardless of the type of change that occurs when heating, cooling, or mixing substances, the total weight of matter is conserved. **5-PS1-4:** Conduct an investigation to determine whether the mixing of two or more substances results in new substances.	Students conduct an investigation where baking soda and vinegar are mixed to learn about the conservation of matter and signs of chemical changes.
Science and Engineering Practices	
Asking questions	Students are engaged in questions about mass and temperature as they carefully test their predictions about observable phenomena.
Planning and carrying out investigations	Students engage in an investigation to gather evidence for whether a chemical reaction occurs when mixing baking soda and vinegar. During the investigation, they collect quantitative and qualitative data concerning mass and temperature.

Continued

Table 11.1. (*continued*)

Matter and Its Interactions	Connections to Classroom Activity
Science and Engineering Practices (*continued*)	
Analyzing and interpreting data	Students analyze changes in data to formulate an evidence-based claim.
Using mathematical and computational thinking	Students measure data to determine whether patterns exist that suggest a relationship.
Constructing explanations	Students construct an evidence-based claim to explain their observations of the law of conservation of mass and indicators of chemical changes.
Disciplinary Core Ideas	
PS1.A: Structure and Properties of Matter: The amount (weight) of matter is conserved when it changes form, even in transitions in which it seems to vanish. **PS1.B:** Chemical Reactions: No matter what reaction or change in properties occurs, the total weight of the substances does not change. (Boundary: Mass and weight are not distinguished at this grade level.)	Students' firsthand experiences with a graduated cylinder–balloon demonstration provide them with evidence that mass is conserved in a chemical reaction.
PS1.B: Chemical Reactions: When two or more different substances are mixed, a new substance with different properties may be formed.	Students' experiences taking the temperature of materials before and after they are mixed provide them with evidence that a change in temperature is a sign of a chemical change.
Crosscutting Concepts	
Patterns	Students look for patterns in data to determine whether a change occurs when baking soda and vinegar are combined.
Cause and effect	Students investigate the relationship between the materials before and after to explain change and the factors that stay the same and different.
Scale, proportion, and quantity	When taking measurements of mass and temperature, students notice that relative information is important at different scales.

Note: The materials, lessons, and activities outlined in this chapter are just one step toward reaching the performance expectations listed in this table. Additional supporting materials, lessons, and activities will be required. See *www.nextgenscience. org/pe/5-ps1-2-matter-and-its-interactions* and *www.nextgenscience.org/pe/5-ps1-4-matter-and-its-interactions* for more information.

Chapter 12

A Natural Storyline for Learning About Ecosystems

Chapter 12

Children are fascinated by nature and come to class having ideas about plants, animals, and their environment. Students' ideas are based on their firsthand experiences. For example, many kids have pets, children's books are abundant with stories about wildlife, and television and children's cartoons often highlight the relationships between people and animals. Capturing students' attention about living things is not difficult; however, students' lived experiences alone do not provide them with comprehensive understandings of living things and their interactions and the basic requirements of life. In this regard, research shows that students have misconceptions about the characteristics used to determine whether something is living as well as about the underlying relationships and interactions of organisms in an environment (Driver et al. 1994).

What follows is a third-grade *explore-before-explain* lesson aimed at developing students' ideas about living things and Earth's systems. As you will see in this lesson, all students are ready to learn at high levels if the content is sequenced in ways where we tap into their prior knowledge and follow up with firsthand explorations that directly relate to their experiences. This lesson is a case in which students' prior experiences directly relate to standards at different grade levels and allow them to explore phenomena in different disciplines. Thus, the storyline includes life science and Earth and space science topics bundled together and begins to address the *Next Generation Science Standards* (*NGSS*) performance expectations (PEs). The PEs include students developing a model to describe the "movement of matter among plants, animals, decomposers, and the environment" (5-LS2-1) and "to describe ways the geosphere, biosphere, hydrosphere, and/or atmosphere interact" (5-ESS2-1; NGSS Lead States 2013).

Also, the activities help students work toward understanding the PE that states they should be able to "construct an argument that plants and animals have internal and external structures that function to support survival, growth, behavior, and reproduction" (4-LS1-1; NGSS Lead States 2013). The idea behind creating storylines for students is that disciplinary core ideas, science and engineering practices, crosscutting concepts, and PEs should be organized in ways to help students develop broader understandings. Rather than approaching learning as a siloed approach and specific to one topic or one discipline at one grade level, we can include ideas that build and support students' past experiences as well as future learning in all science areas to create more coherent frameworks for students trying to understand natural phenomena.

The model lessons include an illustrative example of how to use a formative prior knowledge assessment probe that translates into a firsthand exploration. Students' evidenced-based claims are supported by authoritative explanations using a book and a teacher description to promote more accurate science understanding. All three dimensions of the *NGSS* are easily addressed through the combination of hands-on, minds-on activities (see the table at the end of this chapter).

Assessing Students' Prior Experiences
Engage Phase, Day 1 (25 minutes)
I kicked off the lesson by using a formative prior knowledge assessment probe that was designed to home in on meaningful and relevant phenomena that would be the storyline for our unit exploring life and the interdependence of organisms. We wanted to think about what makes something living and how things are connected in our world in order to maintain life. I used a modified version of the formative assessment probe "Is It Living?" to determine students' experiences (Keeley, Eberle, and Farrin 2005). I purposely focused on ideas in our version of "Is It Living?" that could seamlessly translate into some of our firsthand investigations (see Figure 12.1, p. 120).

I learned from the formative assessment probe that students had different ideas about living versus nonliving and had an incomplete understanding of what factors make some things living versus not living. As my students discussed the reasons for

Chapter 12

Figure 12.1. *The Modified Version of "Is It Living?"*

Listed below are examples of living and nonliving things. Put an X next to the things that could be considered living.

Item Number	Item	Initial	Conversations
1	Tree		
2	Rock		
3	Fire	?	?
4	Wind	?	
5	Grass		
6	Seed		
7	Water	?	
8	Worm		
9	Sun	?	?
10	Snail		

Explain your thinking. What reasoning did you use to decide if something could be living?

Note: **?** = student unsure.

their thinking, they engaged in argumentative discourse where they used logic to try to persuade their peers about their ideas. My role during the conversation was to be a facilitator, and not a judge who evaluated the correctness of ideas and students' logic. I jotted words and notes on the board because the conversation was very fast-paced, and I occasionally asked probing questions to keep the conversation moving along a specific path. For instance, early in our discussion of what makes something living, a student said that "it needs water." I added *water* to the board. The students immediately bought into this idea and wanted to change their initial answers about the wind and water being living and mark them as nonliving.

Another student said that movement was a characteristic of living things. I added the term *movement* to the list. Movement was a tougher defining characteristic for students to use to justify their ideas. For instance, I asked the class, "Do all living things move?" A student said, "Well, plants are living and they don't like to move by themselves. A person can move them. Wind can move them."

The conversations so far about water and moving led directly to discussing fire and the Sun. The students were torn on whether fire and the Sun were living or nonliving based on our list. They went back and forth in their discussion.

Alan: *Fire doesn't need water.*

Janice: *I think it's living* [referring to fire]. *It kinda, like, can spread and move.*

Lisa: *Yeah, it looks like it is alive.*

Janice: *The Sun is living because it's like fire.*

Another student chimed in and changed the direction of the conversation. He said things that are living need food and explained, "Food for grasses would be fertilizer and stuff like that and the dirt. Snails like to eat algae off of plants."

To begin to focus the discussion, we looked at our list, which included water, motion, and food. Students wanted to know if their checklist of living and nonliving things, as well as their characteristics, was correct. I looked at both lists and asked the class, "Can any of the things we identified as living live completely on their own without anything else?" In unison the class said, "No." I asked the same about the things that we thought were nonliving. Before the class could answer, a student said, "A rock is not living and doesn't need anything." At this point, we all agreed that all living things, at some level, need something else that is living (or once living) to survive. This basic idea would be the focus of our exploration.

SAFETY NOTES

1. Wear sanitized, indirectly vented chemical splash safety goggles or safety glasses with side shields and a nonlatex apron during the setup, hands-on, and take-down segments of the activity, for both students and teacher.
2. Use caution when working with sharp objects (e.g., glass or plastic). They can cut or puncture skin.
3. Have direct adult supervision when working on this activity.
4. Immediately wipe up any liquid spilled on the floor—a slip-and-fall hazard.
5. Wash your hands with soap and water after completing this activity.

Exploration

I wanted my students to have experiences with data and models to begin to explore the interdependence of living things. My goal was to test students' ideas and have them explain the closed system in different ways over many days. In this way, I wanted the students to construct knowledge from their experiences, with my role being to introduce scientific terminology and vocabulary in light of their firsthand experiences. I chose to use a bottled ecosystem (designs are abundant on the internet, and there are entire curricula that use 2-liter bottles to model closed ecosystems). We used very simple materials to map out the connectedness among different components of the ecosystem, including snails, worms, aquatic plant bulbs, soil, water, and seeds (see Figure 12.2).

I wanted to include organisms that naturally live together while also being cognizant of the National Science Teaching Association's minimum safety practices and regulations (bottled ecosystems should not

Figure 12.2. *Simple 2-Liter Bottle Ecosystem*

Chapter 12

include vertebrates) (Ingram 1993; see *http://static.nsta.org/pdfs/MinimumSafetyPracticesAndRegulations.pdf*). I provided the students with a list of organisms we would use, and we constructed the bottled ecosystem together. In addition, we purposely created natural habitats that interact, such as terrestrial and aquatic environments. (As a safety note, students' main role was to add the necessary components to the 2-liter system. They have difficulty cutting 2-liter bottles, so I performed this task for them. I took the lead on providing the students with the procedure for constructing the ecosystem.)

Day 2 (25 minutes)

Students eagerly hovered around our ecosystem looking for changes. I wanted to guide them in thinking about the system we were using in our explorations to highlight that scientific models explain, predict, and have limitations (NGSS Lead States 2013). I asked the students to focus their writing in their science notebooks, and to consider their observations and the ways the ecosystem is similar to and different from how these organisms exist in nature.

Figure 12.3. *Condensation Forming on the Bottle*

Figure 12.4. *Drop of Water Accumulating at the Tip of the Straw*

We noticed that one of the first changes was that condensation formed on the bottle and a drop of water accumulated at the tip of the straw (see Figures 12.3 and 12.4). The condensation and water droplets were key sources of evidence for students' construction of knowledge. The students explained that our bottled ecosystem was like nature and the "water is like rain because it goes through the straw and goes back in the water and makes a cycle."

A student also noticed a difference between real-life habitats and our bottled ecosystem. The bottled ecosystem had only a few organisms; as a student explained, "Worms don't live alone in the wild." Thus, the students were realizing that while helping us explain how organisms interact, the bottled ecosystem was a very simplified model of the real world.

Days 3–6 (10–15 minutes a day)

Using the students' science notebooks, we continued collecting data about our ecosystem over the next few days. The students drew pictures of the individual organisms and labeled their specialized parts (4-LS-1; NGSS Lead States 2013). For instance, a student drew a snail and identified that the mouth was specially designed for eating.

I also wanted to focus student thinking on the relationship between living and nonliving things in the ecosystem and to list the materials in both the terrestrial and aquatic habitats. The observation and data collection period reached a new level of enthusiasm when the flowering plants began to sprout (see Figure 12.5).

At this point, I asked students to use arrows to describe how different components were connected. I was pleasantly surprised about what the students were learning about the ecosystem (see Figure 12.6). One student listed his ideas about the system as a whole and wrote "big cycle" and "connected." His list showed how different components of the ecosystem were linked. For instance, his arrows showed that the water plants are connected to the Sun and get water from their aquatic habitat and the snails get food from the water plants. He showed that a straw was used to connect the terrestrial and aquatic habitats and that the aquatic habitat was the water source for the terrestrial environment and the plants buried in the soil (5-ESS2-1; NGSS Lead States 2013).

The sprouting of plants was also a pivotal day for the students' construction of knowledge, and they could make an evidence-based claim about the interdependence of organisms (in other words, their

Figure 12.5. *Plants Begin Sprouting on Day 4*

Figure 12.6. *Student Identifying Connections Between Living and Nonliving Things in the 2-Liter Bottle Ecosystem*

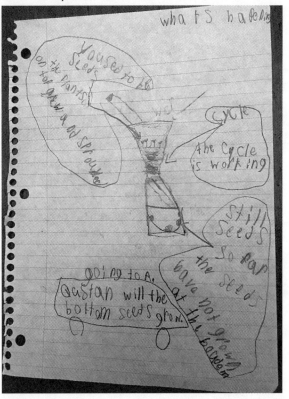

ideas about a "big cycle" and "connected" were related to their observations). What the students did not know was the details of the specific nature of the connections and matter being cycled. We were ready for a more detailed description of how matter cycled through the ecosystems.

Authoritative Explanation (50 minutes)

The purpose of the Explain phase was to introduce new terms and ideas in light of students' firsthand experiences. We kicked off the explanation by reading excerpts from *There's a Hair in My Dirt! A Worm's Story* (Larson 1998). The book introduced a whole host of ideas related to our unit of study. Students learned that "plants did a little more than just make the air crisp and clean—they made the air! Every molecule of oxygen in the Earth's atmosphere was put there by a plant" (Larson 1998, p. 11). I supported the students' developing understanding by having them draw diagrams in their science notebooks with arrows showing that the oxygen produced by plants cycles to the animal life, and the carbon dioxide produced by animals cycles to the plant life. The students also gained a new appreciation for worms when we read the following:

> *Take us worms, for example. We till, aerate, and enrich the earth's soil, making it suitable for plants. No worms, no plants; and no plants, no so-called higher animals running around with their oh-so-precious backbones!* (Larson 1998, p. 52)

We talked about the interactions in the bottled ecosystem and what the students were learning from the reading, and we highlighted three key ideas emphasized by the *NGSS* (NGSS Lead States 2013): (1) Plants are a basic food source for other living organisms; (2) some animals eat plants, and others eat the animals that eat plants; and (3) microscopic bacteria decomposers break down dead organisms as a food source for macroscopic decomposers such as worms. In addition to the students gaining new invertebrate insights, the book validated their evidence-based claims about everything being connected in an ecosystem.

The second portion of the explanation also dealt with cycles, and we made connections between our aquatic and our terrestrial components to Earth's systems. This was a nice tie to Earth and space science. The students had evidence from their experiences that soil, air, and water environments all were necessary components. The students' future experiences would attach scientific terminology to their experiences; the *hydrosphere* helped support life for our plants and animals (*biosphere*), and the *atmosphere* brought water back as *precipitation* (5-ESS2-1; NGSS Lead States 2013). With a basic understanding in place, it was time to see if student understanding transferred to other circumstances.

Elaborate and Evaluate (25 minutes)

The Elaborate phase is dedicated to testing the idea that ecosystems contain organisms that are connected in meaningful ways to sustain life. I asked my students to draw pictures of grass, trees, bugs, birds, and hawks. Next, we cut out the pictures and used them to create and explain a food web. This extension activity asked students to consider a more complex food web (an animal that eats animals) than in our bottled ecosystem. I also asked the students what would happen if the bird were removed from their food web. They realized that the top portion of the food web would be affected if the bird were removed.

The evaluation activities were a chance for me to assess student understanding and for students to think about their developing understanding. The students' answers to the food web in the elaboration activity were my assessment of whether they had gained knowledge of the interdependence of organisms. As a student self-assessment, we went back to their initial ideas about living and nonliving things. The students decided that while the Sun is an essential factor and is integral for life, the Sun and fire are not living things.

While our hands-on experience did not allow students to construct knowledge of the Sun being living versus nonliving, the storyline that the lesson created helped situate the students' learning. Thus, the impact of direct instruction was a particularly potent learning experience and was situated in a broader conceptual framework of life science and Earth and space science. In this way, the students connected the initial assessment probe with their explorations and explanations, and they reflected on their developing understanding.

Conclusions

The most powerful and productive learning environments tap into students' innate abilities and allow them to construct some knowledge from firsthand experiences (National Academies of Sciences, Engineering, and Medicine 2018). While building bottled ecosystems is not a new activity, a way to heighten learning is in the sequence of the assessment probe leading seamlessly to an investigation where students can construct new knowledge. The uniqueness of this lesson is in the research-based instructional sequence that connects well with other topics within a grade level and builds knowledge for future learning. The end result is that students' learning is heightened because they use science practices to construct knowledge based on their firsthand experiences.

See Table 12.1 (p. 126) for the *NGSS* connections visited in this chapter.

Chapter 12

Table 12.1. *Unwrapping the Explore-Before-Explain Ecosystem Lesson*

Ecosystems: Interactions, Energy, and Dynamics and Earth's Systems	Connections to Classroom Activity
Performance Expectations	
5-LS2-1: Develop a model to describe the movement of matter among plants, animals, decomposers, and the environment. **5-ESS2-1:** Develop a model using an example to describe ways the geosphere, biosphere, hydrosphere, and/or atmosphere interact. **4-LS1-1:** Construct an argument that plants and animals have internal and external structures that function to support survival, growth, behavior, and reproduction.	Students used 2-liter bottles to create a closed ecosystem that included two connected components: aquatic and terrestrial environments.
Science and Engineering Practices	
Asking questions and defining problems	Students' predictions about living and nonliving things led to investigative questions about how things interact in an environment.
Planning and carrying out investigations	Students helped build a 2-liter bottle ecosystem to explore how the living and nonliving interact in an ecosystem.
Developing and using models	Students labeled different parts of the 2-liter bottle ecosystem.
Constructing explanations	Students created diagrams to explain how different parts of an ecosystem are related.
Disciplinary Core Ideas	
LS2.A: Interdependent Relationships in Ecosystems: The food of almost any kind of animal can be traced back to plants. Organisms are related in food webs in which some animals eat plants for food and other animals eat the animals that eat plants. Some organisms, such as fungi and bacteria, break down dead organisms (both plants or plants parts and animals) and therefore operate as "decomposers." Decomposition eventually recycles some materials back to the soil. Organisms can survive only in environments in which their particular needs are met. A healthy ecosystem is one in which multiple species of different types are each able to meet their needs in a relatively stable web of life. Newly introduced species can damage the balance of an ecosystem.	Students' firsthand experiences with the bottled ecosystem were connected to what they learned through reading and a teacher explanation. The teacher explanation introduced food webs and decomposers.

Continued

NATIONAL SCIENCE TEACHING ASSOCIATION

Table 12.1. (*continued*)

Ecosystems: Interactions, Energy, and Dynamics and Earth's Systems	Connections to Classroom Activity
Disciplinary Core Ideas (*continued*)	
LS2.B: Cycles of Matter and Energy Transfer in Ecosystems: Matter cycles between the air and soil and among plants, animals, and microbes as these organisms live and die. Organisms obtain gases, and water, from the environment and release waste matter (gas, liquid, or solid) back into the environment.	Students considered the relationship between plants and animals in the bottled ecosystem. They learned from the reading that plants produce oxygen. During the teacher explanation, they created diagrams showing the reciprocal exchange of gases between plants and animals (i.e., plants produce oxygen and animals produce carbon dioxide).
LS1.A: Structure and Function: Plants and animals have both internal and external structures that serve various functions in growth, survival, behavior, and reproduction.	Students closely observed one living thing to describe specific features and their purposes.
ESS2.A: Earth Materials and Systems: Earth's major systems are the geosphere (solid and molten rock, soil, and sediments), the hydrosphere (water and ice), the atmosphere (air), and the biosphere (living things, including humans). These systems interact in multiple ways to affect Earth's surface materials and processes. The ocean supports a variety of ecosystems and organisms, shapes landforms, and influences climate. Winds and clouds in the atmosphere interact with the landforms to determine patterns of weather.	Students learned from their bottled ecosystem that the aquatic habitat provides water for the terrestrial habitat. Earth systems are similar to the 2-liter bottle ecosystem and interact and affect each other in multiple ways.
Crosscutting Concepts	
System and system models	Students used scientific models to explain the interactions that occurred within the bottled ecosystem and make predictions about other examples of ecosystems.
Cause and effect	Students predicted the influence of changing one factor on another in the bottled ecosystem.

Note: The materials, lessons, and activities outlined in this chapter are just one step toward reaching the performance expectations listed in this table. Additional supporting materials, lessons, and activities will be required. For more information, see *www.nextgenscience.org/pe/5-ls2-1-ecosystems-interactions-energy-and-dynamics*, *www.nextgenscience.org/pe/5-ess2-1-earths-systems*, and *www.nextgenscience.org/pe/4-ls1-1-molecules-organisms-structures-and-processes*.

Chapter 13

The Grand Erosion Investigation

Chapter 13

At the beginning of new units of study, teachers have the chance to capture student interest and motivate learning by creating a storyline that drives learning. A storyline is a coherent sequence of activities that is initiated by students' wonder, curiosity, and investigative questions about the world. Storyline teaching is also about opening the learning script to additional standards, in appropriate science disciplines as well as other content areas, to support a fuller understanding of the phenomenon. While this use of storyline teaching can be highly effective, identifying a relevant phenomenon that allows students to ask their investigative questions can be the most challenging part. As a result, there are a growing number of resources that can help teachers use a storyline approach effectively (see *www.nextgenstorylines.org*).

The following is a fourth-grade lesson aimed at helping students explore the *NGSS* performance expectation that states that students should "make observations and/or measurements to provide evidence of the effects of weathering or the rate of erosion by water, ice, wind, or vegetation" (4-ESS2-1; NGSS Lead States 2013). However, to get students to a fuller understanding of this learning objective in a natural example, the lesson bundles together many Earth and space science and life science topics to create a more cohesive storyline for students. The benefit of bundling and including standards from earlier grades is that students deepen understanding because they apply new ideas in different contexts. Because students come from many different classes all with their own unique sets of experiences, this is a way to help them elaborate their earlier learning in a new and different situation that is specific to the current exploration. The hope is that students make connections between old and new learning so they continually expand their understanding and are better able to explain the intricate connections that exist in nature.

The importance of linking new and old ideas in novel situations is based on the research on how students learn best. A hallmark difference between novice and expert learners is that experts can categorize new information and connect it within their existing knowledge of a science phenomenon. Thus, the inclusion of new experiences related to existing ideas develops students' expertise about how the world works (National Academies of Sciences, Engineering, and Medicine 2018). This lesson includes all three dimensions of the *NGSS* (see the table at the end of this chapter) and uses a storyline to structure the 5E (Engage, Explore, Explain, Elaborate, Evaluate) instructional sequence.

Engage

I started the lesson by showing some pictures of the Grand Canyon and asking the class questions about how it could have formed, how old it is, and the types of organisms, if any, that could live in the Grand Canyon. Students had a flurry of ideas. One student thought that the canyon was a result of "plate tectonic" movement. Another wrote "water" and a "river that dried out." The students had a variety of ideas about the age of the Grand Canyon that ranged from 200 to 2,000 to 2 million years old. In terms of life, students thought organisms such as "mountain lions, lizards, and coyotes" lived in the Grand Canyon.

Next, we watching a short video clip about the Grand Canyon so the students could visualize its expansiveness (available at *www.nationalgeographic.com/travel/national-parks/grand-canyon-national-park*). My reason for showing the clip was also to center student thinking and wondering about the river that formed the canyon. With an image of the Grand Canyon in mind, I wanted students to ask questions about the factors that could influence how Earth's materials move. I centered student thinking about "carving out the canyon" and generated possible factors that influence why and how Earth's materials could be moved to carve out a canyon. My goal was to help students understand that scientific questioning often arises out of curiosity and factors that we could test to gain evidence for understanding a phenomenon.[1]

The first brainstorming idea that emerged from our conversation was about water. The students' ideas were logical because of the video, which showed the Colorado River at the bottom of the canyon. I asked the students to draw a model showing how water could create a canyon. Once they created a model, they explained their thinking in a whole-class discussion. One student offered the idea, from her model, about how the force of the water applied (in her words, "how hard the water came down" might influence whether a canyon was formed). Another student suggested, "The amount of water, too, could carve out the canyon." We added these as two separate ideas. The conversation was fast-paced, and I jotted students' ideas on the front board. At the end of the Engage phase, I knew that my students had ideas about how Earth materials may be able to move without specific knowledge of the powerful forces at play that shape our landscape. Thus, the exploration activities were explicitly designed to develop these ideas.

SAFETY NOTES

1. Wear sanitized, indirectly vented chemical splash safety goggles and a nonlatex apron during the setup, hands-on, and take-down segments of the activity, for both students and teacher.
2. Use caution when working with sharp objects (e.g., glassware). They can cut or puncture skin.
3. Have direct adult supervision when doing this activity.
4. Immediately wipe up any liquid spilled on the floor—a slip-and-fall hazard.
5. Wash your hands with soap and water after completing this activity.

Explore (25 minutes)

The Explore phase was dedicated to collecting data and evidence in order to seek answers to our questions. My directions were procedural, and I did not explain the intended content learning goals. I wanted students to be able to focus on their abilities to answer questions from evidence. They worked in groups of three. For each group of three, I cut the top portion out of five 2-liter bottles so each one looked like a boat. Next, we placed the bottles underneath a small piece of wood to raise one end up and lower the other end. Each group received a hand sprayer, a small beaker of water, and a large beaker of water (see Figure 13.1).

---

1. Students asked questions "that can be investigated and predict reasonable outcomes based on patterns such as cause and effect relationships" (NGSS Lead States 2013, p. 4).

Figure 13.1. *Overall Procedural Design for the Grand Erosion Investigation*

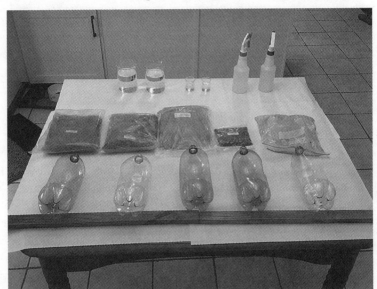

Then, the students filled each of the 2-liter bottles with the different types of Earth materials (sand, sandy soil, red clay, pebbles, and loam) (see Figure 13.2). I told the students to fill them full enough that the Earth materials reached the height of the pouring spout on the bottle (see Table 13.1, p. 134, for notes on preparation). We performed our investigations on white paper on our tabletops. The exploration could easily be conducted outside.

Figure 13.2. *Student Filling a Bottle With Red Clay Soil*

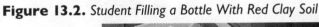

Chapter 13

Table 13.1. *Notes on Preparation*

We conducted the investigation on our tabletops, and I placed white butcher paper down to keep the tabletops as clean as possible. I placed the Earth materials on a table in the center of the room so everyone could retrieve them. (In hindsight, I would advise teachers to perform the investigation outdoors.)

Figure 13.3. *Student Simulating Rain on Fine Sand*

The first tests that students performed were to use the spray bottles to simulate rainfall and to test whether rain could break down the Earth material or move it to form a canyon. The spray bottles allowed for a whole host of tests, and the students were encouraged to adjust their spray settings to explore many different possible conditions. Before we delved into the exploration, I had the students fill their bottles with 350 ml of water.

The exploration was guided, and together we explored how applying a mist was different from a spray flow with more force. In addition, we tested how changing the amount of sprays, as well as pouring entire volumes of water from our beakers, influenced the movement of the Earth materials from a more quantitative perspective. Thus, the students engaged in science and engineering practices related to carrying out an investigation and analyzing and interpreting data. They were using the data from different tests, and analyzing their observations, to reveal patterns that indicate a relationship (see Figures 13.3 and 13.4).[2]

Figure 13.4. *Students Simulating Rain on the Sandy Soil and the Red Clay*

The students quickly came to some scientific revelations, and they were surprised when certain materials broke down while others remained intact.[3] Almost immediately, a student called me over when using her spray bottle and said, "Look, I'm making a mini canyon" in the red clay. Another student remarked, "I'm

2. Students "conduct an investigation collaboratively to produce data to serve as the basis for evidence" and "make observations and /or measurements to produce data to serve as evidence for an explanation of phenomena" (NGSS Lead States 2013, p. 7).

3. Students analyze and interpret data to make sense of phenomena (NGSS Lead States 2013, p. 9).

making a canyon in the loam." This was a time when students' observations allowed them to compare and contrast the causal relationship between Earth material types and the application of water to the system.

Students quickly learned that how much Earth material moved was dependent on both the force and the amount of water applied. The students could see that they were able to carve out a path in the sand, sandy soil, red clay, and loam but not in the pebbles. In addition, they gained a whole new appreciation for how much material moves when they poured water more forcefully and in higher concentrations (a YouTube video illustrating this part of the exploration can be found at *https://youtu.be/kiXhV9lfYXE*). The loam was most easily displaced when water was more forcefully added to the bottle (see Figure 13.5).

At the end of the water investigation, the students were able to make their first evidence-based claim: The water simulating rain broke down certain materials (red clay soil and loam), carved out a path in other materials (sand and sandy soil), and did nothing to others (pebbles).[4]

Figure 13.5. *Loam Being Moved From the Bottle*

Students' firsthand experiences also related well to their models as we compared and contrasted their initial conceptions with their experiences in the investigation. While the students had ideas about water moving Earth's materials, they were enlightened by how impactful a spray that consisted only of a mist could be on the system. Students commented that they were "surprised that a little mist could break down and move the red clay." They gained a whole new appreciation for water's role in the movement of Earth's materials and the fact that, like the mist that broke down and moved red clay, a light rain could have a similar influence in natural environments.

Explain (two 25-minute lessons)

Our data were qualitative, and the combination of hands-on, minds-on experiences allowed students to construct knowledge of Earth's processes that was directly related to our overarching phenomenon—the formation of the Grand Canyon. The first portion of the explanation was dedicated to reading *Grand Canyon* by Jason Chin (2017). I read the book out loud to the students, who were eager to make connections between their hands-on experiences and more sophisticated understanding. As an added benefit, the students were engaged in the type of reading highlighted by the *Common Core State Standards for English Language Arts* (*CCSS ELA*) related to using informational texts as a source of information and research (CCSS.ELA-Literacy.W.4.9; National Governors

4. Students "construct an explanation of the relationship" between the amount of water and force of water and the movement of Earth's materials (NGSS Lead States 2013, p. 11).

Chapter 13

Association Center for Best Practices and Council of Chief State School Officers 2010). We were just one page into the reading when the terms *erosion* and *weather* were introduced along with their role in the formation of the Grand Canyon. The context of the reading provided clues to these terms' meanings, and we would revisit the particulars of their importance at the end of the Explain phase.

The students were intrigued by so many topics that were connected to ideas we would talk about this year and that were connected to their prior experiences. The book did an excellent job of helping them develop a more elaborate understanding of several life and Earth science topics that they learned about in earlier grades (see Table 13.2).

Table 13.2. *Connections Between the Reading and Earlier Learning and Performance Expectations*

Ideas Promoted in the Reading	Performance Expectations
Students were surprised that frogs lived in the canyon, and this changed their view of its only being desertlike. They gained a new and different example of the relationship between the nuances of a habitat and an organism's ability to survive that was contextualized by their experiences with the storyline approach.	**3-LS4-3:** Construct an argument with evidence that in a particular habitat some organisms can survive well, some survive less well, and some cannot survive at all.
Students were unsure of the immense amount of time it took the canyon to form. They learned that its creation took billions of years versus the 200 that some students thought. Thus, students had a specific example of how slowly some Earth events occur.	**2-ESS1-1:** Use information from several sources to provide evidence that Earth events can occur quickly or slowly.
Students learned about how fossils found in the canyon provide evidence of life from a previous time. Students were stunned that in earlier times, the Grand Canyon was underwater, as evidenced by fossil life found in the canyon's rock layers. Although students had previously learned about fossils, they had another example that was specific to the Grand Canyon.	**3-LS4-1:** Analyze and interpret data from fossils to provide evidence of the organisms and the environments in which they lived long ago.

Note: For more information, see *www.nextgenscience.org/pe/3-ls4-3-biological-evolution-unity-and-diversity, www.nextgenscience.org/pe/2-ess1-1-earths-place-universe,* and *www.nextgenscience.org/pe/3-ls4-1-biological-evolution-unity-and-diversity.*

One end result of the reading was that the class was developing connections between prior experiences and new information that was situated in learning about the Grand Canyon. For teachers, the bundling of both new and old standards is one way to create more conceptual coherence and a richer storyline for students. At the end of the read-out-loud, I wanted students to internalize the most salient points for them from the reading. The students completed a summarizing sheet called "Be the Teacher!" (see Figure 13.6).

Figure 13.6. *Student's Responses to the "Be the Teacher!" Summarizing Sheet*

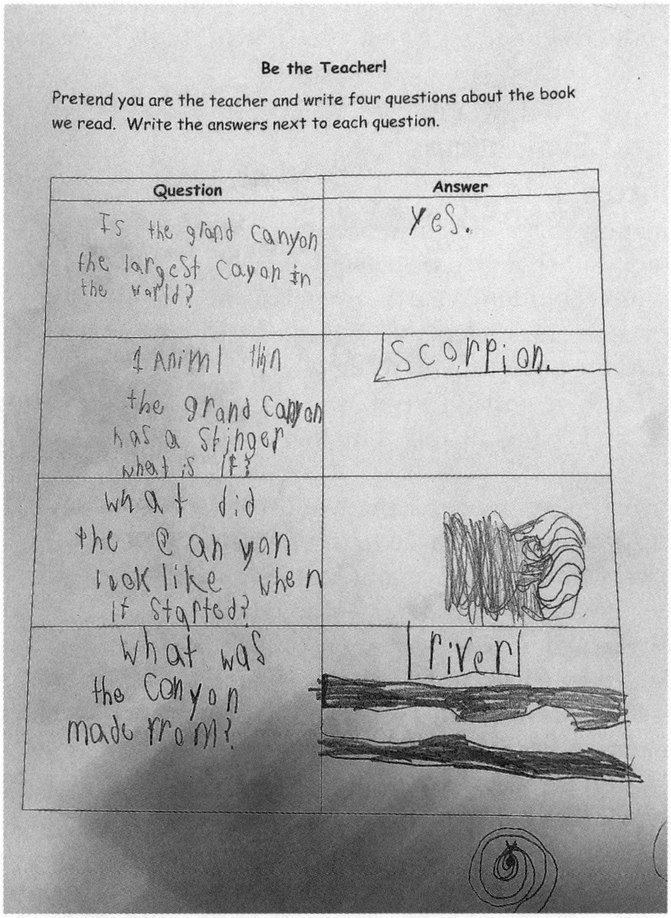

Be the Teacher!

Pretend you are the teacher and write four questions about the book we read. Write the answers next to each question.

Question	Answer
Is the grand canyon the largest cayon in the world?	yes.
1 animl thin the grand canyon has a stinger what is it?	scorpion.
what did the canyan look like when it started?	
what was the canyon made from?	river

After the reading activity, I wanted to hook scientific terminology to evidence and experiences that the students had with their firsthand explorations and with the reading. I revisited the terms *weather* and *erosion* and described the process of land breaking down due to natural causes. I asked students for examples of when they used water to break apart the land in our investigation. They said, "The water broke down both clay soil and loam." I also asked the students to provide examples of when the

Chapter 13

Earth materials were taken away by water. They made connections between when water was forcefully applied and moving the material out of the 2-liter bottle's spout.

The final conversation that ensued was targeted at explaining reasons for why weather and erosion occur. The students had many ideas, including "when weaker soil types are broken into smaller pieces by water, the smaller parts can easily be moved by water." At the end of the explanation, the students connected all three activities in the lesson covered so far—the video, the firsthand exploration, and the reading—and concluded that both erosion and weather contributed to the formation of the Grand Canyon.[5]

Elaboration and Evaluations (two 25-minute sessions)

The final investigation was all about broadening our understanding of weather and erosion and investigating whether wind could move Earth's materials in a similar way as water. The students were challenged with the task of carving out a canyon using wind. We placed different Earth materials (sand, sandy soil, red clay, pebbles, and loam) in foil containers (see Figure 13.7).

The students worked in groups of three and blew through straws to simulate wind. I asked them to blow through the straws with different amounts of force. (*Note*: The teacher should warn students not to inhale through the straw.) See Figure 13.8.

Similar to the students' experiences with water, they learned that the force of wind directly influences certain Earth materials' abilities to move.[6] Unlike with the use of water, the sand and sandy soil were readily moved by wind (a video on moving sand and sandy soil is available on YouTube at *https://youtu. be/3rs5leJmj88*). The red clay was partially moved by wind. Both the loam and the pebbles were unaffected by our wind source. The students were able to compare and contrast the water and wind explorations to

Figure 13.7. *Earth Materials Set Up for Exploring Wind*

Figure 13.8. *Student Simulating Wind on Earth Materials*

5. Students used the crosscutting concept of cause and effect to "identify and test causal relationships and use these relationships to explain" the relationship between weathering and erosion and the formation of the Grand Canyon (NGSS Lead States 2013, p. 5).

6. Students "conduct an investigation collaboratively to produce data to serve as the basis for evidence" (NGSS Lead States 2013, p. 7).

realize that whether a specific type of Earth material is displaced depends on the properties of the material.[7]

The final activity was a time to consider our developing understanding and see what we had learned about the Grand Canyon and Earth's processes. I included students in the evaluation phase, and they worked with partners to quiz each other using the "Be the Teacher!" activity. While my assessment of their conceptual knowledge took place, and I evaluated their evidence-based claims, the students were excited to test each other's factual knowledge.

Conclusions

Using phenomena when creating a storyline encourages students to wonder about their world and seek answers through evidence-based experiences. As illustrated in the Grand Erosion Investigation, many science disciplines contribute to an elaborated understanding of the concepts. As students construct knowledge of the target ideas, they simultaneously develop ideas about related topics. In this way, the students are gaining a more realistic appreciation for the special combination that exists within and between science disciplines, as well as in other areas (in this case, ELA), and the fact that the most authentic learning environments include knowledge in many domains.

See Table 13.3 for the *NGSS* connections visited in this chapter.

Table 13.3. *Unwrapping the* Explore-Before-Explain *Erosion Lesson*

Earth's Systems	Connections to Classroom Activity
Performance Expectation	
4-ESS2-1: Make observations and/or measurements to provide evidence of the effects of weathering or the rate of erosion by water, ice, wind, or vegetation.	Students explore the influence of wind and water on weather and erosion for different Earth materials.
Science and Engineering Practices	
Asking questions and defining problems	Students ask questions about how water and wind influence the movement of sand, sandy soil, red clay, pebbles, and loam.
Planning and carrying out investigations	Students use water to simulate rain and blow through a straw to simulate wind to test the influence of these forces on the movement of Earth materials.

Continued

---

7. Students were able to "analyze and interpret data to make sense of phenomena" to construct an evidence-based claim (NGSS Lead States 2013, p. 9).

Table 13.3. (*continued*)

Earth's Systems	Connections to Classroom Activity
Science and Engineering Practices (*continued*)	
Analyzing and interpreting data	Students analyze qualitative data as evidence for the relationship between applying water and wind to different Earth materials and whether they move from place to place.
Constructing explanations	Students create evidence-based claims about the factors that can make Earth materials move.
Disciplinary Core Idea	
ESS2.A: Earth Materials and Systems: Rainfall helps to shape the land and affects the types of living things found in a region. Water, ice, wind, living organisms, and gravity break rocks, soils, and sediments into smaller particles and move them around.	Students' firsthand experiences moving Earth materials with water and wind are connected to what they learned in the read-out-loud and from the explanation of weathering and erosion.
Crosscutting Concepts	
Cause and effect	Students infer a causal relationship between Earth's materials and the forces that move them to better understand how the Grand Canyon was formed.
Scale, proportion, and quantity	Students learn that there are many relative factors at play, and the time to form the canyon, the size of particles affecting the rate of erosion, and the energy difference for varying amounts or rates of water flow must all be contextualized in a broader understanding of specific scales, time frames, and quantities.

Note: The materials, lessons, and activities outlined in this chapter are just one step toward reaching the performance expectation listed in this table. Additional supporting materials, lessons, and activities will be required. For more information, see *www.nextgenscience.org/pe/4-ess2-1-earths-systems*.

Chapter 14

Leadership and Lessons Learned

Chapter 14

Educators—and, specifically, teachers—make the difference in science classrooms. If you have embraced the ideas presented so far, you are joining a growing community of science educators who realize that better preparation of students in schools also makes a difference in society. The lessons shared up until this point are preparing you to lead the way to the future for your students and even your colleagues. Now is a time to ask yourself: Are you ready to up the level of the challenge I first proposed in the introduction and spread the word about *explore-before-explain* teaching to other teachers?

Explore-before-explain teachers know something not yet understood by others. To be an effective *explore-before-explain* teacher, you must integrate what you know about instructional activities, content, and learners in a very intricate and organized manner. Scholars have termed the important and specialized type of knowledge necessary for effective teaching *pedagogical content knowledge* (PCK; see Gess-Newsome 1999). PCK symbolizes a powerful type of professional knowledge achieved through the integration of many different domains (i.e., pedagogy, content, and learners). High levels of PCK are imperative for quality teaching and are necessary to ensure that students develop deep science understanding.

If you are wondering why some teachers never become *explore-before-explain* teachers, it is intimately tied to their PCK. I have worked with many well-intentioned teachers whose orientations toward science teaching and knowledge in one or more areas (i.e., content, learners and learning, or pedagogy) hindered their ability to implement 5E (Engage, Explore, Explain, Elaborate, Evaluate) or POE (Predict, Observe, and Explain) instructional sequences. However, by developing their knowledge in these areas and thus gaining higher levels of PCK, they were better able to be *explore-before-explain* teachers. Being acutely aware, motivated, and determined to work to develop research-based professional practice develops teachers' PCK and is crucial to effective teaching.

Working with students and teachers has allowed me to think about best practices in new and different ways. I have learned quite a bit about teacher knowledge, science teaching, and teacher professional development. In this final chapter, I share some lessons learned so you can pave the way for translating the *Next Generation Science Standards* (*NGSS*; NGSS Lead States 2013) into practice not only for your students but also for your colleagues.

Lesson 1: Focus on Science Phenomena That Students Can Explain From Firsthand Experiences

Keep in mind that excellent, well-designed instruction matters most. Science teaching requires the careful consideration of students' ideas, including misconceptions, and the types of activities that lead toward accurate understanding. When designing 5E and POE lessons, home in on science experiences that allow students to make accurate evidence-based claims. The knowledge that students construct from direct experiences is powerful and long-lasting. Students' experiential learning becomes the foundation of their knowledge. Finding the focus requires us to think deeply about the content, the activities, and our students.

Once foundations are created, all other topics and ideas within the unit of study can be connected to students' experiences. In the process, key associated ideas are tied to students' developing knowledge while other nonessential topics are cut. Instructional planning around phenomena is considered a "depth versus breadth" approach to teaching, which is all about highlighting in our teaching what we want students to know and remember in the long term to gain higher levels of scientific literacy. Using a depth versus breadth approach keeps instruction focused on big ideas and their relationship to phenomena and not on science factoids. The result is that students learn and retain the key ideas in science that are important for explaining the world they live in.

Having well-developed content knowledge and a solid understanding of how ideas are connected within a discipline is critical to being an *explore-before-explain* teacher. This requires us to have in-depth content knowledge and to be able to organize knowledge in such a way that all of the desired learning outcomes are directly linked to the phenomena that students explore firsthand. Remember, deeper content knowledge is worth developing and is a critical piece of a teacher's PCK.

Lesson 2: Emphasize an *Explore-Before-Explain* Learning Orientation With Students

Young kids come to school with a natural curiosity about how the world works. However, many students enter classes where the teacher's focus on covering content supersedes fostering questioning and thinking abilities. Many students are taught science in a traditional way instead of exploring it first for themselves. The pressure that some teachers feel about covering content to make students more academic may be counterproductive, because it may narrow the range of learning activities that kids are willing to consider, it does not encourage the cognitive work they are capable of doing, and it does not prepare them for deeper knowledge building in the future. Building deep understanding requires treating science learning as a coherent progression over time and across science disciplines.

Explore-before-explain learning requires risk taking and an uninhibited sense of wonder about the world. Students need supportive environments that encourage exploration. Children need to believe that their ideas, in all forms and stages of development, are valued. In this process, students should be encouraged to test hypotheses against evidence; make causal inferences; and use statistics, data, and probability models to explain phenomena. Focusing on valid and reliable means of collecting and interpreting data versus concentrating on whether ideas are "good" or not is a way to highlight the importance of thinking like scientists.

Always remember that *A Framework for K–12 Science Education* (*Framework*; National Research Council 2012) emphasizes the interconnectedness of content, thinking, and

Chapter 14

doing. The science and engineering practices (SEPs), crosscutting concepts (CCs), and disciplinary core ideas are most effectively intertwined in such a way that one strand alone is best learned in concert with the others, and no one strand is more important than another. Although grappling with data and evidence might be challenging, and although students may need guidance in how to think logically about their experiences, students need to achieve success forming evidence-based claims. Carefully sequencing activities so they lead to the desired outcome is one way to help students form accurate evidence-based claims. Reflection on learning can be a powerful motivator in helping students become learners who are more self-sufficient.

Having a deep understanding of students' intellectual abilities and sequences of instruction also helps teachers assist students in becoming learners who are more self-reliant. Knowledge of learners and pedagogy (e.g., instructional sequence) is foundational to being an *explore-before-explain* teacher and is central to PCK development.

Lesson 3: Planning *Explore-Before-Explain* Lessons Naturally Incorporates Many SEPs and CCs

In an era of science education reform, it can be difficult to plan three-dimensional instructional lessons and curricula. In fact, many teachers (and districts) spend countless hours (and professional development funds) learning new standards and attempting to put the vision of reform into practice. Some teachers and districts are successful, while others are not. One way to adapt to new standards as proposed by the *Framework* and the *NGSS* is to use tried-and-true, research-based instructional sequences to teach science.

Using the POE and 5E models allows teachers to easily incorporate many SEPs and CCs during all phases of instruction. Whether you are a teacher or a professional developer looking to update the science curriculum, the POE and 5E models allow for more standards-based teaching. Both of these approaches have stood the test of time. Their roots can be traced back to the late 1960s and the Science Curriculum Improvement Study learning cycle, so although the standards might change over time, the proven benefits of *explore-before-explain* instructional sequences can provide the infrastructure necessary to design more standards-based lessons.

The model lessons in this book are excellent examples of how 5E and POE instructional sequences allow teachers to include SEPs and CCs called for by the *Framework* and the *NGSS*. Remember, the *Framework* and the *NGSS* are research-based documents. Much of the research that supports them also directly supports *explore-before-explain* instructional sequences. Developing curricular knowledge (e.g., knowledge of standards) and its connection to instructional sequence is an important step in becoming an *explore-before-explain* teacher and is imperative to developing higher levels of PCK.

Lesson 4: Becoming an *Explore-Before-Explain* Teacher Does Not Happen Overnight

The process of conceptual change is similar for students and teachers. The process of changing our beliefs about instructional practice can be difficult because we are not aware of our own misconceptions about teaching. There are rational (and sometimes irrational) reasons why we do not change our practices. Change is hard because we have very well-formed views of what good teaching looks like.

You may not have realized this, but we started our teaching internships as kindergarten students. Our experiences in schools as students helped shape our beliefs about teaching science. Dan Lortie (1975) argued that firsthand experiences can complicate teacher learning about educational practices. A shift from traditional teaching to *explore-before-explain* practices may be counterintuitive for a whole host of reasons. Many of us were successful students, and our achievements established firm beliefs about teaching. These assertions are supported by my own research, in which I learned that teachers' images of teachers and beliefs about teaching might act as a barrier to change by limiting the ideas they are willing to entertain (see Brown, Friedrichsen, and Abell 2013). As a result, the design practices involved with creating 5E and POE lessons could be considerably different from our firsthand experiences learning science. Remember, your students are not you, and what motivated you in science may be different from your students' interests.

In addition, keep in mind that there are many different types of conceptual change, and some are more challenging to overcome than others. Conceptual change requires knowledge to be restructured by breaking and making new connections among the types of exploratory experiences that we want students to have to form explanations. For some, the new connections may be an elaboration on ideas you already had about effective teaching. Others may be at a critical juncture. Conceptual change involves thinking about teaching and learning in very different and new ways. Because of the complexity of this process, we are likely to require time, well-supported opportunities, and examples to work with and try out with students.

Taking our knowledge of learning to new levels requires us to know, embrace, and design instruction based on the current understanding of cognition and of how to sequence science instruction so students learn best. Developing our knowledge of the most effective learning and teaching methods based on research is a way to increase PCK.

Lesson 5: Teachers Overcome Misconceptions About 5E and POE Sequences When They Understand the Research and Theory Supporting These Approaches

Many teachers have misconceptions about what 5E and POE instructional sequences are and how they work. Although model lessons can provide activities that increase motivation and heighten understanding, teachers benefit from a more research-based understanding of the sequence of activities that produces the most optimal learning conditions. Using the model lessons in and of themselves without understanding the theoretical underpinnings will most likely not be enough to help you become an *explore-before-explain* teacher. The importance of educational research and theory in informing the design of 5E and POE instructional sequences cannot be overstated.

The first set of teachers' misconceptions deals with interpreting the phase names of models such as the POE and 5E in a trivial sense versus being grounded in the research literature. For instance, teachers may think the purpose of the Engage phase is only to hook students into the lesson and motivate learning. Although this is one purpose of the engagement phase, of equal importance is identifying students' prior knowledge, including misconceptions. A strong finding from the cognitive science research and conceptual change theory is that learning is built on the foundation of existing knowledge and understanding. To ignore the role of prior knowledge in *explore-before-explain* instructional sequences would violate indispensable conditions for effective learning.

Another common misconception concerns the Explain phase. Some teachers believe that once they have come to this phase, it is their chance to describe and tell students about the scientific phenomenon. While teacher-provided explanations are important in teaching, the Explain phase should begin with students' evidence-based claims of the phenomenon under study. Students' explanations are pivotal and represent the knowledge they have constructed and will serve as the foundation for their learning.

A third common misconception regards the Evaluate phase. Some teachers believe that evaluation is a chance to finally assess student understanding. In fact, throughout *explore-before-explain* instructional sequences, teachers use formative assessment to scaffold student learning. Assessment is important at every phase of learning. In this process, it is important also to promote students' self-assessment of knowledge. The Evaluate phase provides students a chance to look inward, reflect, and think about how their knowledge has grown through changes, elaborations, and additions over time—in other words, metacognition. Promoting metacognition helps students take more control over their learning, and it is an important aspect of how they learn best (Bransford, Brown, and Cocking 2000).

These are just a few of the most common misconceptions I have encountered when offering professional development for teachers at all career stages—from teacher candidate to experienced teacher—that can act as a barrier to developing more research-based practices.

The second set of *explore-before-explain* instructional sequence misconceptions deals with the arrangement and order of phases. Some teachers have trouble letting students explore science before they explain new ideas. They want to provide mini-lessons to introduce new terms and concepts and then start with the engagement or prediction phase. Introducing new terms and concepts before students have begun building a framework for understanding science phenomena can be counterproductive to developing a deeper understanding of these ideas. Teachers need to remember that terms, concepts, and new ideas connect to the knowledge that students have constructed firsthand. Providing new terms out of context creates the risk that these ideas will not be learned or remembered. Many times, these mini-lessons need to be retaught so that students will make meaningful connections between new terms and science phenomena. Although the choice of hands-on activity (e.g., lab, demonstration) and the means by which teacher explanations are provided (e.g., lectures, readings, videos) depend on our resources and abilities, the sequence of *explore-before-explain* must be intact for optimum learning to occur for most students.

The model lessons in this book are only a few from the large corpus of examples of *explore-before-explain* lessons used to teach science. Although model lessons can be a great way to increase student learning, motivation, and understanding of science content and practices, they in themselves do not prepare instructors to be *explore-before-explain* teachers. Understanding the extensive research should serve as the backbone for designing *explore-before-explain* instructional sequences. Always keep in mind that how we structure practice is key to what students remember. Understanding the scholarship on learning and cognition is critical to developing higher levels of PCK and being *explore-before-explain* teachers.

Conclusions

As you have seen throughout this book, thinking deeply about all facets of learning and sequencing science instruction is both fascinating and eye-opening. I hope that the activities here have raised fundamental questions about your students and the activities you use when teaching science. Many teachers who have switched to 5E and POE instructional sequences have developed their professional knowledge of learning and teaching, and their PCK, in important ways:

- Increased their knowledge of student ideas and misconceptions
- Deepened their understanding of activities that promote accurate evidence-based claims
- Enhanced their ability to co-construct knowledge with students about scientific principles that are not easily accessible firsthand
- Elaborated, refined, and developed their understanding of content
- Expanded their understanding of student difficulties in learning content
- Heightened their knowledge of students' ideas about the nature of science
- Amplified their knowledge of effective instructional sequences
- Grown their knowledge of instructional activities that conform to specific phases of instruction
- Advanced their understanding of connections within and among topics, ideas, and concepts in science and overall content knowledge

Chapter 14

I hope that the model lessons, research, and tips for designing research-based sequences of science instruction motivate you to use the 5E and POE models in science teaching. Starting the journey of becoming an *explore-before-explain* teacher is a rewarding professional process that forces you to consider the best possible environments to ensure that students gain high levels of learning. Your students will benefit from a more robust and relevant understanding of science and will organize their understandings based on direct experiences. I encourage you to create foundational situations for students that allow them to construct knowledge of science phenomena with data and evidence based on firsthand experiences. I wish you the best of luck as you develop 5E and POE instructional sequences to take student learning to new levels in your classrooms and schools.

References

Abell, S. K., and M. J. Volkmann. 2006. *Seamless assessments in science: A guide for elementary and middle school teachers.* Arlington, VA: NSTA Press.

Abraham, M. R. 1992. Instructional strategies designed to teach science. In *Research matters … to the science teacher*, ed. F. Lawrenz, K. Cochran, J. Krajcik, and P. Simpson, 41–50. Manhattan, KS: NARST Monograph #5.

ACT. 2015. ACT introduces new STEM college readiness benchmark; Results reveal limited readiness for college STEM coursework. ACT, Inc. *www.act.org/content/act/en/newsroom/act-introduces-new-stem-college-readiness-benchmark--results-rev.html.*

American Association for the Advancement of Science (AAAS). 1993. *Benchmarks for science literacy.* New York: Oxford University Press.

American Association for the Advancement of Science and Project 2061. n.d. Pilot and field test data collected between 2006 and 2010. Unpublished raw data. *http://assessment.aaas.org.*

Atkin, J. M., and R. Karplus. 1962. Discovery or invention? *The Science Teacher* 29: 45–47.

Banilower, E., K. Cohen, J. Pasley, and I. Weiss. 2010. *Effective science instruction: What does research tell us?* 2nd ed. Portsmouth, NH: RMC Research Corporation Center on Instruction.

Blakemore, S.-J. 2010. The developing social brain: Implications for education. *Neuron* 65 (6): 744–747.

Blakemore, S.-J., and S. Choudhury. 2006. Development of the adolescent brain: Implications for executive function and social cognition. *Journal of Child Psychology and Psychiatry* 47 (3–4): 296–312.

Bobrowsky, M., M. Korhonen, and J. Kohtamaki. 2014. *Using physical science gadgets and gizmos, grades 6–8: Phenomenon-based learning.* Arlington, VA: NSTA Press.

Bransford, J., A. Brown, and R. Cocking. 2000. *How people learn: Brain, mind, experience, and school.* Washington, DC: National Academies Press.

Brown, P., and S. Abell. 2007a. Cultural diversity in the science classroom. *Science and Children* 44 (9): 60–61.

Brown, P., and S. Abell. 2007b. Examining the learning cycle. *Science and Children* 44 (5): 58–59.

Brown, P., and S. Abell. 2008a. Project-based science and the elementary classroom. *Science and Children* 45 (4): 60–61.

References

Brown, P., and S. Abell. 2008b. Using social issues in science class. *Science and Children* 64 (8) 64–65.

Brown, P., P. Friedrichsen, and S. Abell. 2013. The development of prospective secondary biology teachers' PCK. *Journal of Science Teacher Education* 24 (1): 133–155.

Bybee, R. W. 1997. *Achieving scientific literacy: From purposes to practices.* Portsmouth, NH: Heinemann Educational Books.

Bybee, R. W., ed. 2002. *Learning science and the science of learning.* Arlington, VA: NSTA Press.

Bybee, R. W. 2012. Scientific and engineering practices in K–12 classrooms: Understanding *A Framework for K–12 Science Education. The Science Teacher* 78 (9): 34–40.

Bybee, R. W. 2015. *The BSCS 5E Instructional Model: Creating teachable moments.* Arlington, VA: NSTA Press.

Bybee, R. W., J. A. Taylor, A. Gardner, P. Van Scotter, J. C. Powell, A. Westbrook, and N. Landes. 2006. *The BSCS 5E instructional model: Origins, effectiveness, and applications.* Colorado Springs, CO: BSCS. *https://media.bscs.org/bscsmw/5es/bscs_5e_full_report.pdf.*

Chin, J. 2017. *Grand Canyon.* New York: Roaring Brook Press.

Contant, T. L., J. L. Bass, A. A. Tweed, and A. A. Carin. 2018. *Teaching science through inquiry-based instruction.* 13th ed. Carmel, IN: Pearson.

Donovan, M. S., and J. D. Bransford, eds. 2005. *How students learn: Science in the classroom.* National Research Council Committee on How People Learn: A targeted report for teachers. *www.nap.edu/catalog/11102/how-students-learn-science-in-the-classroom.*

Driver, R., A. Squires, P. Rushworth, and V. Wood-Robinson. 1994. *Making sense of secondary science: Research into children's ideas.* London: Routledge.

Duschl, R. A. 2012. The second dimension: Crosscutting concepts. *The Science Teacher* 79 (2): 34–38.

Duschl, R. A., H. A. Schweingruber, and A. W. Shouse, eds. 2007. *Taking science to school: Learning and teaching science in grades K–8.* Washington, DC: National Academies Press.

Eisenkraft, A. 2003. Expanding the 5E model: A proposed 7E model emphasizes "transfer of learning" and the importance of eliciting prior understanding. *The Science Teacher* 70 (6): 56–59.

Ericsson, K. A., N. Charlness, P. J. Feltovich, and R. R. Hoffman, eds. 2006. *The Cambridge handbook of expertise and expert performance.* Cambridge, UK: Cambridge University Press.

Gess-Newsome, J. 1999. PCK: An introduction and orientation. In *Examining PCK: The construct and its implications for science education,* ed. J. Gess-Newsome and N. Lederman, 3–20. Boston: Kluwer.

Gopnik, A., A. Meltzoff, and P. K. Kuhl. 1999. *The scientist in the crib: Minds, brains, and how children learn.* New York: William Morrow.

Hattie, J. A. C. 2009. *Visible learning: A synthesis of over 800 meta-analyses relating to achievement.* London: Routledge.

Haysom, J., and M. Bowen. 2010. *Predict, observe, explain: Activities enhancing student understanding.* Arlington, VA: NSTA Press.

Hofstein A., and V. N. Lunetta. 2004. The laboratory in science education: Foundation for the 21st century. *Science Education* 88 (1): 28–54.

Ingram, M. 1993. *Bottle biology.* Dubuque, IA: Kendall/Hunt.

International Association for the Evaluation of Educational Achievement (IEA). 2015. TIMSS & PIRLS International Study Center. Boston College, Lynch School of Education. *https://nces.ed.gov/timss/timss2015.*

Karplus, R., and H. D. Their. 1967. *A new look at elementary school science.* Chicago: Rand McNally.

Keeley, P. 2019. Apple in the dark: Formative assessment probes and misconceptions. *Science and Children* 56 (5): 15–17.

Keeley, P., F. Eberle, and C. Dorsey. 2008. *Uncovering student ideas in science, Volume 3: Another 25 formative assessment probes.* Arlington, VA: NSTA Press.

Keeley, P., F. Eberle, and L. Farrin. 2005. *Uncovering student ideas in science, Volume 1: 25 formative assessment probes.* Arlington, VA: NSTA Press.

Keeley, P., F. Eberle, and J. Tugel. 2007. *Uncovering student ideas in science, Volume 2: 25 more formative assessment probes.* Arlington, VA: NSTA Press.

Keeley, P., and J. Tugel. 2009. *Uncovering student ideas in science, Volume 4: 25 new formative assessment probes.* Arlington, VA: NTSA Press.

Koch, J. 2018. *Science stories: Science methods for elementary and middle school teachers.* 6th ed. Boston: Cengage Learning.

Krajcik, J. S., S. Codere, C. Dahsah, R. Bayer, and K. Mun. 2014. Planning instruction to meet the intent of the *Next Generation Science Standards. Journal of Science Teacher Education* 25 (2): 157–175.

Larson, G. 1998. *There's a hair in my dirt! A worm's story.* New York: HarperCollins Publishers.

Lortie, D. 1975. *Schoolteacher: A sociological study.* Chicago: University of Chicago Press.

References

Maurer, T. 2013. *The scoop about measuring matter*, ed. S. Duke. Vero Beach, FL: Rourke Educational Media.

McNeill, K. L., and J. Krajcik. 2012. *Supporting grade 5–8 students in constructing explanations in science: The claim, evidence, and reasoning framework for talk and writing.* New York: Pearson.

Michaels, S., A. W. Shouse, and H. A. Schweingruber. 2008. *Ready, set, science! Putting research to work in K–8 science classrooms.* Washington, DC: National Academies Press. *www.nap.edu/catalog/11882/ready-set-science-putting-research-to-work-in-k-8#toc.*

National Academies of Sciences, Engineering, and Medicine (NASEM). 2018. *How people learn II: Learners, contexts, and cultures.* Washington, DC: National Academies Press.

National Governors Association Center for Best Practices and Council of Chief State School Officers (NGAC and CCSSO). 2010. *Common Core State Standards.* Washington, DC: NGAC and CCSSO.

National Research Council (NRC). 1996. *National science education standards.* Washington, DC: National Academies Press.

National Research Council (NRC). 2012. *A framework for K–12 science education: Practices, crosscutting concepts, and core ideas.* Washington, DC: National Academies Press.

NGSS Lead States. 2013. *Next Generation Science Standards: For states, by states.* Washington, DC: National Academies Press..

O'Brien, T. 2010. *Brain-powered science: Teaching and learning with discrepant events.* Arlington, VA: NSTA Press.

O'Brien, T. 2011a. *Even more brain-powered science: Teaching and learning with discrepant events.* Arlington, VA: NSTA Press.

O'Brien, T. 2011b. *More brain-powered science: Teaching and learning with discrepant events.* Arlington, VA: NSTA Press.

Organisation for Economic Co-operation and Development. 2012. OECD Programme for International Student Assessment. *www.oecd.org/pisa.*

Padilla, M. J., I. Miaoulis, and M. Cyr. 2007. *Science explorer: Physical science.* Boston: Pearson Prentice Hall.

Posner, G. J., K. A. Strike, P. W. Hewson, and W. A. Gertzog. 1982. Accommodation of a scientific conception: Toward a theory of conceptual change. *Science Education* 66 (2): 211–227.

Reiser, B. J. 2013. What professional development strategies are needed for successful implementation of the Next Generation Science Standards? Paper prepared for K–12 Center at ETS Invitational Symposium on Science Assessment, Washington, DC. *www.ets.org/Media/Research/pdf/reiser.pdf.*

Singer, S. R., M. L. Hilton, and H. A. Schweingruber, eds. 2006. *America's lab report: Investigations in high school science.* Washington, DC: National Academies Press.

Stepans, J. 1996. *Targeting students' science misconceptions: Physical science concepts using the conceptual change approach.* Riverview, FL: Idea Factor.

Stiles, J., and T. L. Jernigan. 2010. The basics of brain development. *Neuropsychology Review* 20 (4): 327–348.

U.S. Department of Education. 2015. The Nation's Report Card. Institute of Education Sciences, National Center for Education Statistics. *www.nationsreportcard.gov/science_2015/#?grade=4.*

Wiggins, G., and J. McTighe. 2005. *Understanding by design.* Expanded 2nd ed. Alexandria, VA: ASCD.

Index

Page numbers printed in **boldface type** indicate tables or figures.

Index

Index

NATIONAL SCIENCE TEACHING ASSOCIATION

Index